Instant Vorte Recipes

100 Instant Vortex Air Fryer Recipes To Lose Weight

ZOE BAKER

Table of Content

BREAKFAST

Baked Potato Breakfast Boats

Basic Recipe

Preparation Time: 10 minutes **Cooking Time:** 20 minutes **Serving:** 4

INGREDIENTS:

- 2 large russet potatoes, scrubbed
- Olive oil
- Salt
- Freshly ground black pepper
- 4 eggs
- 2 tablespoons chopped, cooked bacon
- 1 cup shredded cheddar cheese

DIRECTIONS:

1. Poke holes in the potatoes with a fork and microwave on full power for 5 minutes. Turn potatoes over and cook an additional 3 to 5 minutes, or until the potatoes are fork tender.
2. Cut the potatoes in half lengthwise and use a spoon to scoop out the inside of the potato. Be careful to leave a layer of potato so that it makes a sturdy —boat.lLightly spray the fryer basket with olive oil. Spray the skin side of the potatoes with oil and sprinkle with salt and pepper to taste.
3. Place the potato skins in the fryer basket skin side down. Crack one egg into each potato skin.
4. Sprinkle ½ tablespoon of bacon pieces and ¼ cup of shredded cheese on top of each egg. Sprinkle with salt and pepper to taste.
5. Air fry until the yolk is slightly runny, 5 to 6 minutes, or until the yolk is fully cooked, 7 to 10 minutes

NUTRITION: Calories 338 Fat15g Saturated Fat 8g Cholesterol 214mg Carbs 35g Protein 17g Fiber 3g Sodium: 301mg

Greek Frittata

Intermediate Recipe Preparation Time: 10
minutes **Cooking Time:** 20 minutes **Serving:** 4

INGREDIENTS:

- Olive oil
- 5 eggs
- ¼ teaspoon salt
- ⅛ Teaspoon freshly ground black pepper
- 1 cup baby spinach leaves, shredded
- ½ cup halved grape tomatoes
- ½ cup crumbled feta cheese

DIRECTIONS:

1. Spray a small round air fryer-friendly pan with olive oil.
2. In a medium bowl, whisk together eggs, salt, and pepper and whisk to combine.
3. Add the spinach and stir to combine.
4. Pour ½ cup of the egg mixture into the pan.
5. Sprinkle ¼ cup of the tomatoes and ¼ cup of the feta on top of the egg mixture.
6. Cover the pan with aluminum foil and secure it around the edges.
7. Place the pan carefully into the fryer basket.
8. Air fry for 12 minutes
9. Remove the foil from the pan and cook until the eggs are set, 5 to 7 minutes
10. Remove the frittata from the pan and place on a serving platter. Repeat with the remaining ingredients.

NUTRITION: Calories 146 Fat 10g Saturated Fat 5g Cholesterol 249mg Carbs 3g Protein 11g Fiber 1g Sodium: 454mg

Mini Shrimp Frittata

Intermediate Recipe Preparation Time: 15 minutes **Cooking Time:** 20 minutes **Serving:** 4

INGREDIENTS:

- 1 teaspoon olive oil, plus more for spraying
- ½ small red bell pepper, finely diced
- 1 teaspoon minced garlic
- 1 (4-ounce) can of tiny shrimp, Dry out
- Salt
- Freshly ground black pepper
  - 4 eggs, beaten
  - 4 teaspoons ricotta cheese

DIRECTIONS:

1. Spray four ramekins with olive oil. In a medium skillet over medium-low heat, heat 1 teaspoon of olive oil. Add the bell pepper and garlic and sauté until the pepper is soft, about 5 minutes
2. Add the shrimp, season with salt and pepper, and cook until warm, 1 to 2 minutes Remove from the heat.
3. Add the eggs and stir to combine. Pour one quarter of the mixture into each ramekin.
4. Place 2 ramekins in the fryer basket and cook for 6 minutes. Remove the fryer basket from the air fryer and stir the mixture in each ramekin. Top each frittata with 1 teaspoon of ricotta cheese. Return the fryer basket to the air fryer and cook until eggs are set and the top is lightly browned, 4 to 5 minutes
5. Repeat with the remaining two ramekins.

NUTRITION: Calories 114 Fat 7g Carbs 1g Protein 12g

Spinach and Mushroom Mini Quiche

Intermediate Recipe Preparation Time: 10 minutes **Cooking Time:** 15 minutes **Serving:** 4

INGREDIENTS:

- 1 teaspoon olive oil, plus more for spraying
- 1 cup coarsely chopped mushrooms
- 1 cup fresh baby spinach, shredded
- 4 eggs, beaten
- ½ cup shredded Cheddar cheese
- ½ cup shredded mozzarella cheese
- ¼ teaspoon salt
- ¼ teaspoon black pepper

DIRECTIONS:

1. Spray 4 silicone baking cups with olive oil and set aside. In a medium sauté pan over medium heat, warm 1 teaspoon of olive oil. Add the mushrooms and sauté until soft, 3 to 4 minutes
2. Add the spinach and cook until wilted, 1 to 2 minutes Set aside.
3. In a medium bowl, whisk together the eggs, Cheddar cheese, mozzarella cheese, salt, and pepper. Gently fold the mushrooms and spinach into the egg mixture.
4. Pour ¼ of the mixture into each silicone baking cup. Place the baking cups into the fryer basket and air fry for 5 minutes Stir the mixture in each ramekin slightly and air fry until the egg has set, an additional 3 to 5 minutes

NUTRITION: Calories 183 Fat 13g Saturated Fat 7g Cholesterol 206mg Carbs 3g Protein 14g Fiber 1g Sodium: 411mg

Italian Egg Cups

Basic Recipe
Preparation Time: 5 minutes
Cooking Time: 10 minutes

Serving: **4**
INGREDIENTS:

- Olive Oil
- 1 cup marinara sauce
- 4 eggs
- 4 tablespoons shredded mozzarella cheese
- 4 teaspoons grated Parmesan cheese
- Salt
- Freshly ground black pepper
- Chopped fresh basil, for garnish

DIRECTIONS:

1. Lightly spray 4 individual ramekins with olive oil.
2. Pour ¼ cup of marinara sauce into each ramekin.
3. Crack one egg into each ramekin on top of the marinara sauce.
4. Sprinkle 1 tablespoon of mozzarella and 1 tablespoon of Parmesan on top of each egg. Season it with salt and pepper.
5. Cover each ramekin with aluminum foil. Place two of the ramekins in the fryer basket.
6. Air fry for 5 minutes and remove the aluminum foil. Air fry until the top is lightly browned and the egg white is cooked, another 2 to 4 minutes If you prefer the yolk to be firmer, cook for 3 to 5 more minutes
7. Repeat with the remaining two ramekins. Garnish with basil and serve.

NUTRITION: Calories 135 Fat 8g Saturated Fat 3g Cholesterol 191mg Carbs 6g Protein 10g Fiber 1g Sodium: 407mg

Mexican Breakfast Pepper Rings

Basic Recipe

Preparation Time: 5 minutes **Cooking Time:**
10 minutes **Serving**: 4 **INGREDIENTS:**

- Olive oil
- 1 large red, yellow, or orange bell pepper, cut into four ¾-inch rings
- 4 eggs
- Salt
- Freshly ground black pepper
- 2 teaspoons salsa

DIRECTIONS:

1. Lightly spray a small round air fryer–friendly pan with olive oil.
2. Place 2 bell pepper rings on the pan. Crack one egg into each bell pepper ring. Season it with salt and black pepper.
3. Spoon ½ teaspoon of salsa on top of each egg. Place the pan in the fryer basket. Air fry until the yolk is slightly runny, 5 to 6 minutes or until the yolk is fully cooked, 8 to 10 minutes
4. Repeat with the remaining 2 pepper rings. Serve hot.
5. Pair It With: Turkey sausage or turkey bacon make this a heartier morning meal.
6. Air Fry Like A Pro: Use a silicone spatula to easily move the rings from the pan to your plate.

NUTRITION: Calories 84 Fat 5g Saturated Fat 2g Cholesterol 186mg Carbs 3g Protein 7g Fiber 1g Sodium: 83mg

Cajun Breakfast Muffins

Intermediate Recipe Preparation Time: 10 minutes
Cooking Time: 10 minutes **Serving**: 6

INGREDIENTS:

- Olive oil
- 4 eggs, beaten
- 2¼ cups frozen hash browns, thawed
- 1 cup diced ham
- ½ cup shredded Cheddar cheese
- ½ teaspoon Cajun seasoning

DIRECTIONS:

1. Lightly spray 12 silicone muffin cups with olive oil.
2. In a medium bowl, mix together the eggs, hash browns, ham, Cheddar cheese, and Cajun seasoning in a medium bowl.
3. Spoon a heaping 1½ tablespoons of hash brown mixture into each muffin cup.
4. Place the muffin cups in the fryer basket.
5. Air fry until the muffins are golden brown on top and the center has set up, 8 to 10 minutes
6. Make It Even Lower Calorie: Reduce or eliminate the cheese.

NUTRITION: Calories 178 Fat 9g Saturated Fat 4gCholesterol 145mg Carbs 13g Protein 11g Fiber 2g Sodium: 467mg

Hearty Blueberry Oatmeal

Intermediate Recipe Preparation Time: 10 minutes
Cooking Time: 25 minutes **Serving**: 6

INGREDIENTS:

- 1½ cups quick oats
- 1¼ teaspoons ground cinnamon, divided
- ½ teaspoon baking powder
- Pinch salt
- 1 cup unsweetened vanilla almond milk
- ¼ cup honey
- 1 teaspoon vanilla extract
- 1 egg, beaten
- 2 cups blueberries
- Olive oil
- 1½ teaspoons sugar, divided
- 6 tablespoons low-fat whipped topping (optional)

DIRECTIONS:

1. In a large bowl, mix together the oats, 1 teaspoon of cinnamon, baking powder, and salt.
2. In a medium bowl, whisk together the almond milk, honey, vanilla and egg.
3. Pour the liquid ingredients into the oats mixture and stir to combine. Fold in the blueberries.
4. Lightly spray a round air fryer–friendly pan with oil.
5. Add half the blueberry mixture to the pan.
6. Sprinkle ⅛ teaspoon of cinnamon and ½ teaspoon sugar over the top.
7. Cover the pan with aluminum foil and place gently in the fryer basket. Air fry for 20 minutes remove the foil and air fry for an additional 5 minutes Transfer the mixture to a shallow bowl.
8. Repeat with the remaining blueberry mixture, ½ teaspoon of sugar, and ⅛ teaspoon of cinnamon.
9. To serve, spoon into bowls and top with whipped topping.

NUTRITION: Calories 170 Fat 3g Saturated Fat 1g Cholesterol 97mg Carbs 34g Protein 4g Fiber 4g Sodium: 97mg

Banana Bread Pudding

Intermediate Recipe Preparation Time: 10 minutes **Cooking Time:** 20 minutes **Serving:** 4

INGREDIENTS:

- Olive oil
- 2 medium ripe bananas, mashed
- ½ cup low-fat milk
- 2 tablespoons peanut butter
- 2 tablespoons maple syrup
- 1 teaspoon ground cinnamon
- 1 teaspoon vanilla extract
- 2 slices whole-grain bread, torn into bite-sized pieces
- ¼ cup quick oats

DIRECTIONS:

1. Lightly spray four individual ramekins or one air fryer–safe baking dish with olive oil.
2. In a large mixing bowl, combine the bananas, milk, peanut butter, maple syrup, cinnamon, and vanilla. Using an electric mixer or whisk, mix until fully combined.
3. Add the bread pieces and stir to coat in the liquid mixture.
4. Add the oats and stir until everything is combined.
5. Transfer the mixture to the baking dish or divide between the ramekins. Cover with aluminum foil.
6. Place 2 ramekins in the fryer basket and air fry until heated through, 10 to 12 minutes
7. Remove the foil and cook for 6 to 8 more minutes
8. Repeat with the remaining 2 ramekins. Make It Even Lower Calorie: Reduce the calories by using sugar-free maple syrup or by replacing the peanut butter with PB2 (powdered peanut butter). Combine 4 tablespoons of powdered peanut butter with 2 tablespoons of water to equal 2 tablespoons of peanut butter.

NUTRITION: Calories 212 Fat 6g Saturated Fat 2g Carbs 38g Protein 6g Sodium: 112mg

Air fried German Pancakes

Basic Recipe

Preparation Time: 5 minutes **Cooking Time:** 8 Minutes **Serving**: 5 **INGREDIENTS:**

- Serving size: 1/2 cup batter
- 3 Full eggs
- Whole wheat flour: 1 cup
- Almond milk: 1 cup
- A pinch of salt
- Apple sauce: 2 heaping tablespoons (optional but recommended to replace the need for added oil or butter)
- For Garnishing:
- Berries
- Greek yogurt
- Confectioner sugar
- Maple syrup (optional)

DIRECTIONS:

1. Set the air fryer temperature to 390°F/199°C. Inside the air fryer, set the cast iron tray or ramekin as it heats. Take the blender and add all the batter ingredients to it, and combine until smooth. If the batter is too thick, simply add milk or applesauce tablespoons to smooth out. Use nonstick baking spray and spray the cast iron tray or ramekin, and then dump in a batter serving.
2. Air fry the batter for 6-8 minutes
3. Do not worry if top gets hard to touch. This is the advantage of using the air fryer – it provides the pancake with a good firm outer coating/edges that softens as it cools. Place the remaining batter in the refrigerator in an airtight container to freshen it up every morning.
4. Garnish, and serve.

NUTRITION: Calories 139 Protein 8 g Fat 4 g Carbs 18 g
Fiber 3 g Sugar 1 g

Air-Fried Flax Seed French toast Sticks with Berries

Intermediate Recipe Preparation Time: 25 minutes **Cooking Time:** 35 minutes **Serving:** 4

INGREDIENTS:

- Whole-grain bread: 4 slices (1 1/2-oz.)
- 2 Big Eggs
- 1/4 cup 2% reduced-fat milk
- Vanilla extract: 1 teaspoon
- Ground cinnamon: ½ teaspoon
- 1/4 cup of light brown sugar, split,
- 2/3 cup flax seed cooking spray
- 2 Cups of fresh-cut strawberries
- Maple syrup: 8 teaspoons
- Powdered sugar: 1 teaspoon

DIRECTIONS:

1. Cut each of the bread slices into four long sticks. In a shallow dish, whisk together eggs, milk, cinnamon, vanilla extract, and 1 tablespoon brown sugar. In a second, shallow dish, combine flaxseed meal and remaining 3 tablespoons of brown sugar.
2. Dip the pieces of bread in a mixture of eggs, soak them slightly, and allow any excess to drip away. Dredge each piece in a mixture of flax seeds and coat on all sides. Cover the bits of bread with cooking oil.
3. Place pieces of bread in a single layer in the air fryer basket, leave room between each piece and cook at 375 ° F in batches until golden brown and crunchy,
   10 minutes, turn slices over halfway through cooking. Place 4 sticks of French toast on each plate to serve. Finish with 1/2 cup of strawberries, 2 teaspoons of maple syrup, and a powdered sugar layer. Serve right now.

NUTRITION: Calories 361 Fat 10g Saturated Fat 1g Unsaturated Fat 7g Protein 14g Carbs 56g Fiber 10g Sugars: 30g Sodium: 218mg

Breakfast Frittatas

Basic Recipe

Preparation Time: 15 minutes **Cooking Time:**
20 minutes **Serving:** 2

INGREDIENTS:

- Breakfast sausage: ¼ pound, completely cooked and crumbled
- Eggs: 4, lightly beaten
- Shredded cheddar cheese: ½ cup
- Red pepper: 2 tablespoons, chopped
- Green onion: 1 chopped
- Cayenne pepper: 1 pinch
- Cooking spray

DIRECTIONS:

1. Combine the sausage, eggs, cheddar cheese, onion, bell pepper, and cayenne in a bowl and blend. Set the temperature of the air-fryer to 360°F (180°C). Sprinkle a 6x2-inch non-stick cake pan with a cooking spray.
2. Put the mixture of the eggs in the prepared cake pan. Cook in the air fryer for 18 to 20 minutes until the frittata is set.

NUTRITION: Calories 379.8 Protein 31.2g Carbs 2.9g Cholesterol 443mg Sodium: 693.5mg

Air-Fried Breakfast Bombs

Basic Recipe

Preparation Time: 20 minutes **Cooking Time:**
5 minutes **Serving:** 2

INGREDIENTS:

- Bacon: 3 slices, center-cut
- 3 Big, lightly beaten eggs
- 1 1/3-ounce fat cream cheese, softened
- Fresh chives: 1 tablespoon, chopped
- 4 Ounces of new whole wheat flour pizza dough

- Cooking spray

DIRECTIONS:

1. Cook the bacon over medium to very crisp in a medium skillet, around 10 minutes Take bacon off the pan. In a pan, add eggs to the bacon drippings; cook for about 1 minute, frequently stirring, until almost set, but still loose. Transfer eggs to a bowl; add cream cheese, chives, and crumbled bacon to taste.

2. Divide the dough into four pieces equal to each. Roll each piece into a 5-inch circle onto a lightly floured surface—place one-fourth of each dough circle in the middle of the egg mixture. Brush the outside edge of the dough with water; wrap the dough around the mixture of the eggs to form a bag, pinch the dough at the seams together.

3. In air fryer tray, put dough bags in a single layer; coat thoroughly with cooking spray. Cook for 5 to 6 minutes at 350 ° F until golden brown, then test for 4 minutes

Nutrition: Calories 305 Fat 15g Saturated fat 5g Unsaturated fat 8g Protein 19g Sodium 548mg Calcium 5% DV Potassium 2% DV
Carbs 26g Fiber 2g Sugars 1g Added sugars 0g

Banana Bread

Basic Recipe

Preparation Time: 5 minutes **Cooking Time:** 30 minutes **Serving:** 4

Ingredients:

- Banana: 1, ripe and mashed
- 1 egg
- Brown sugar: 2-3 tablespoons
- Canola oil: 2 tablespoons
- Milk: 1/4 cup
- Plain flour: ¾ cup mixed with 1/2 tablespoon baking soda

DIRECTIONS:

1. Whisk the egg into the mashed banana in a small bowl. Add the sugar, butter, and milk and whisk again.
2. Add the flour and baking soda in the mixture and blend until mixed.
3. If using an air fryer, preheat for 3 minutes to 320°F/160°C.
4. Pour the batter into the dish of air fryer (apply a little butter on the basket) and cook for 32 to 35 minutes, or until a toothpick inserted into the cake's bottom comes out clean. A touch of stickiness is all right.
5. Let the tin/dish cool for 10 minutes, then transfer to a wire rack to cool down.

NUTRITION: Calories 233 kcal Carbs 34g Sugar: 13g Vitamin A: 105IU Cholesterol 42mg Sodium: 25mg Protein 5g Fat 9g Saturated Fat 1g Potassium: 178mg Fiber 1g Vitamin C: 2.6mg Calcium: 34mg Iron: 1.4m

SNACK

Cheesy Garlic Sweet Potatoes

Basic Recipe

Preparation Time: 10 minutes **Cooking Time:**
25 minutes **Servings:** 4 **INGREDIENTS:**

- Sea salt
- ¼ cup garlic butter melts
- ¾ cup shredded mozzarella cheese
- ½ cup of parmesan cheese freshly grated
- 4 medium sized sweet potatoes
- 2 tsp freshly chopped parsley

DIRECTIONS:

1. Heat the oven to 400 degrees Fahrenheit and brush the potatoes with garlic butter and season each with pepper and salt. Arrange the cut side down on a greased baking sheet until the flesh is tender or they turn golden brown.
2. Remove them from the oven, flip the cut side up and top up with parsley and parmesan cheese.
3. Change the settings of your instant fryer oven to broil and on medium heat add the cheese and melt it. Sprinkle salt and pepper to taste. Serve them warm

NUTRITION: Calories 321 Fat 9g, Carbs 13g, Proteins 5g,

Crispy Garlic Baked Potato Wedges

Basic Recipe

Preparation Time: 5 minutes **Cooking Time:** 10 minutes **Servings:** 3 **INGREDIENTS:**

- 3 tsp salt
- 1 tsp minced garlic
- 6 large russets
- ¼ cup olive oil
- 1 tsp paprika
- 2/3 finely grated parmesan cheese
- 2 tsp freshly chopped parsley

DIRECTIONS:

2. Preheat the oven into 350 degrees Fahrenheit and line the baking sheet with a parchment pepper.
3. Cut the potatoes into halfway length and cut each half in half lengthways again. Make 8 wedges.
4. In small jug combine garlic, oil, paprika and salt and place your wedges in the baking sheets. Pour the oil mixture over the potatoes and toss them to ensure that they are evenly coated.
5. Arrange the potato wedges in a single layer on the baking tray and sprinkle salt and parmesan cheese if needed. Bake it for 35 minutes turning the wedges once half side is cooked. Flip the other side until they are both golden brown. Sprinkle parsley and the remaining parmesan before serving.

NUTRITION: Calories, 289 Fat 6g Carbs 8g Proteins 2g

Sticky Chicken Thai Wings

Basic Recipe

Preparation Time: 10 minutes **Cooking Time:** 30 minutes **Servings:** 6 **INGREDIENTS:**

- 3 pounds chicken wings removed
- 1 tsp sea salt to taste
- For the glaze:
- ¾ cup Thai sweet chili sauce
- ¼ cup soy sauce
- 4 tsp brown sugar
- 4 tsp rice wine vinegar
- 3 tsp fish sauce
- 2 tsp lime juice
- 1 tsp lemon grass minced
- 2 tsp sesame oil
- 1 tsp garlic minced

DIRECTIONS:

6. Preheat the oven to 350 degrees Fahrenheit. Lightly spray your baking tray with cooking tray and set it aside. To prepare the glaze combine the ingredients in a small bowl and whisk them until they are well combined. Pour half of the mixture into a pan and reserve the rest.

7. Trim any excess skin off the wing edges and season it with pepper and salt. Add the wings to a baking tray and pour the sauce over the wings tossing them for the sauce to evenly coat. Arrange them in a single layer and bake them for 15 minutes

8. While the wings are in the oven, bring your glaze to simmer in medium heat until there are visible bubbles.

9. Once the wings are cooled on one side rotate each piece and Bake it for an extra 10 minutes baste them and return them into the oven to allow for more cooking until they are golden brown. Garnish with onion slices, cilantro, chili flakes. Sprinkle the remaining salt. Serve it with glaze of your choice.

NUTRITION: Calories 246 Fat 16g Carbs 19g Proteins: 20g

Coconut Shrimp

Basic Recipe

Preparation Time: 15 minutes **Cooking Time:** 15 minutes **Servings**: 6 **INGREDIENTS:**

- Salt and pepper
- 1-pound jumbo shrimp peeled and deveined
- ½ cup all-purpose flour
- For batter:
- ½ cup beer
- 1 tsp baking powder
- ½ cup all-purpose flour
- 1 egg
- For coating:
- 1 cup panko bread crumbs
- 1 cup shredded coconut

DIRECTIONS:

10. Line the baking tray with parchment paper. In a shallow bowl add ½ cup flour for dredging and in another bowl whisk the batter ingredients. The batter should resemble a pancake consistency. If it is too thick add a little mineral or beer whisking in between. In another bowl mix together the shredded coconut and bread crumbs.

11. Dredge the shrimp in flour shaking off any excess before dipping in the batter and coat it with bread crumb mixture. Lightly press the coconut into the shrimp. Place them into the baking sheet and repeat the process until you have several.

12. In a Dutch oven skillet heat vegetable oil until it is nice and hot fry the frozen shrimp batches for 3

minutes per side. Dry out them on a paper towel lined plate. Serve immediately with sweet chili sauce.

NUTRITION: Calories 287 Fat 11g Carbs 46g Proteins 30g

Spicy Korean Cauliflower Bites

Basic Recipe

Preparation Time: 15 minutes **Cooking Time:**
30 minutes **Servings:** 4 **INGREDIENTS:**

- 2 eggs
- 1 lb. cauliflower
- 2/3 cups of corn starch
- 2 tsp smoked paprika
- 1 tsp garlic grated
- 1 tsp ginger grated
- 1 lb. panko
- 1 tsp sea salt
- For the Korean barbecue sauce
- 1 cup ketchup
- ½ cup Korea chili flakes
- ½ cup minced garlic
- ½ cup red pepper

DIRECTIONS:

1. Cut the cauliflower into small sizes based on your taste and preference.
2. In a small bowl add cornstarch and eggs and mix them until they are smooth.
3. Add onions, garlic, ginger, smoked paprika and coat them with panko.
4. Apply some pressure so that the panko can stick and repeat this with all the cauliflower.
5. Set your vortex to 400 degrees Fahrenheit for a half an hour. Line your tray with aluminum foil or parchment paper and use nonstick spray to cover it.
6. When the vortex plus BEEPS _add food' put your food and set the timer to 30 minutes or choose a program that will automatically choose the duration the food will take to cook. In the middle of the cooking the appliance will beep again to indicate turn food. You will take it out and flip it for the other side to cook well.
7. While it is cooking for the second part you can begin preparing your spicy Korean barbecue sauce.
8. Sauté the ingredients and Drizzle with the oil at the bottom. Fry the garlic for a minute before adding all the remaining ingredients and simmering

it for 15 minutes

9. Keep it warm and serve with your cauliflower bites.

NUTRITION: Calories 118 Fat 2g Carbs 21g Proteins 4g

Mini Popovers

Basic Recipe

Preparation Time: 10 minutes **Cooking Time:** 15 minutes **Servings:** 4 **INGREDIENTS:**

- 1 tsp butter melted
- 2 eggs at room temperature
- 1 cup of milk at room temperature
- 1 cup all-purpose flour
- Salt and pepper to taste

DIRECTIONS:

10. Generously coat a mini popover with nonstick spray.
11. Add all the ingredients to a blender and process it at medium speed.
12. Fill each mold with 2 tsp batter. Place a drip pan at the bottom of the cooking chamber.
13. Using the display panel selects AIRFRY and adjusts it to 400 degrees Fahrenheit and a time of 20 minutes then touch START.
14. When the display panel indicates _add food' place the egg bite mold on the lower side of the cooking tray. When the display indicates —TURNFOOD‖ do not touch anything. When the popovers are brown open the cooking chamber and pierce them to release steam and cook for a minute or so.
15. Serve immediately.

NUTRITION: Calories53 Fat 1g Carbs 9g Proteins 2g

Dehydrated Spiced Cauliflower

Basic Recipe

Preparation Time: 10 minutes **Cooking Time:**
1 hour **Servings:** 3 **INGREDIENTS:**

- ½ tsp nutmeg
- 2 lb. head of cauliflower
- 1 tsp olive oil
- 1 tsp smoked paprika
- 1 tsp hot sauce
- 1 tsp lime juice
- 1 tsp cumin

DIRECTIONS:

16. Chop the cauliflower into tiny sizes that can fit on your thumb. In your large bowl combine cauliflower and the remaining ingredients and toss to coat them evenly.
17. Divide the cauliflower and make an even layer in a baking tray. Place a drip pan at the bottom of the cooking chamber and insert a tray at the top most position and another at the bottom.
18. Used the display panel and choose DEHYDRATE and adjust the temperature to 130 degrees and touch START. When the dehydration processes are over, Press START again and removes the popcorn and serve immediately.

NUTRITION: Calories 30 Fat 2g Carbs 3g Proteins 0g

Instant Vortex plus Asparagus

Basic Recipe

Preparation Time: 10 minutes **Cooking Time:** 30 minutes **Servings:** 4 **INGREDIENTS:**

- 1 tsp extra virgin oil
- 1 lb. asparagus
- ½ tsp kosher salt
- Salt and pepper to taste

DIRECTIONS:

1. Set your instant vortex plus to AIRFRY at 400- degree Fahrenheit. The preheating process will begin and you can also begin to prepare the asparagus.
2. Cut the woody ends about 2 inches off the bottom of the asparagus and coat them with oil before seasoning with salt and pepper.
3. When the instant vortex is ready carefully open its door and use the silicone mitt to pull the tray before loading the asparagus and closing the door.
4. The appliance will automatically begin the cooking process and it will beep halfway through to allow you to flip the food and allow the asparagus to cook further. Once you have cooked the asparagus and is ready.
5. Serve while hot with a sauce of your choice

NUTRITION: Calories 136 Fat 12g Carbs 4g Proteins 3g

Roasted Ranch Potatoes

Basic Recipe

Preparation Time: 5 minutes **Cooking Time:** 15
minutes **Servings:** 2 **INGREDIENTS:**

- 1 tsp olive oil
- 1 ½ dry ranch seasoning and salad dressing mix
- 1.5 lbs. of potatoes

DIRECTIONS:

19. Cut the potatoes into 1-inch chunk, for smaller potatoes you can cut them into quarters.
20. Rinse the potato chunks in cold water and place them in a plate with paper towels. This is effective because it will help in reducing water in the potatoes.
21. Toss the potatoes in seasoning and preheat your air fryer
22. Once the air fryer has attained the right temperature it is time to load it with the potatoes. Add the potatoes at 380 degrees Fahrenheit.
23. Cook the potatoes for 7 minutes before flipping them and cooking them again for another 7 minutes your fryer should be on baking mode.
24. Once the potatoes are golden brown, remove them and serve with a sauce of your choice.

NUTRITION: Calories 231 Fat 7g Carbs 37 Proteins 5g

Herbed Turkey Breast with Gravy

Intermediate Recipe Preparation Time: 10 minutes
Cooking Time: 40minutes **Servings:** 4
INGREDIENTS:

- 1 tsp fresh thyme
- 3 tsp unsalted butter
- 1 tsp fresh safe
- 1 tsp fresh rosemary leaves
- Fully grated lemon zest
- 2 tsp kosher salt
- 2 cloves garlic
- Freshly ground pepper
- For the gravy
- 4 tsp unsalted butter
- ¼ cup all-purpose flour
- 2 ½ cups chicken broth
- Salt and pepper to taste

DIRECTIONS:

25. Make the turkey by placing 3 tsp of unsalted butter in a bowl and allowing it to melt at room temperature. Prepare 1 tsp fresh thyme leaves, 1 tsp rosemary leaves, 1 tsp sage, 1 tsp grated lemon zest, 2 minced garlic cloves.
26. Add a teaspoon of kosher salt and ground black pepper before smashing everything together into a paste.
27. Pat the turkey dry with paper towels before loosening its skin. Spread the butter mixture in an even layer all over the skin of the chicken. Season the turkey with the remaining 1 tsp of kosher salt, and ½ tsp of ground black pepper.
28. Line your baking tray with a parchment paper or a baking sheet. Set the appliance to 350 degrees Fahrenheit and set the cook time to 40 minutes Place the turkey skin side down on the rack and push start button on the panel. Allow the turkey to cook for 20 minutes before flipping the other side to cook as well.
29. While the other part of the turkey is cooking make the gravy by melting 4 tsp of unsalted butter in a pan and whisk ¼ cup of flour and cook it for 3 minutes cooking it continuous before adding chicken stock.

Simmer until the gravy has thickened well. Taste and season, it with salt and pepper until the turkey is amazing.

30. Serve while hot.

NUTRITION: Calories 296.9 Fat 16.9g Carbs 3.3g Proteins 32.9g

Apple Cider Donuts

Basic Recipe

Preparation Time: 25 minutes **Cooking Time:**
45 minutes **Servings:** 6 **INGREDIENTS:**

- 3 cups all-purpose flour
- 2 cups apple cider
- ½ cup light brown sugar
- 2 tsp baking powder
- 1 tsp ground cinnamon
- 1 tsp ground ginger
- 8 tsp unsalted butter
- ½ tsp baking soda
- 1 tsp kosher salt

    - For finishing:
    - ¼ cup all-purpose flour
    - 8 tsp unsalted butter
    - 1 cup granulated sugar
    - 1 tsp cinnamon

DIRECTIONS:

31. Pour 2 cups of apple cider into a pan and bring it to boil transfer the reduced apple dicer once it is half the volume and allow it to cool completely.
32. Put 3 cups all-purpose flour, ½ cup brown sugar, 1 tsp ground cinnamon, 2 tsp baking soda, ½ tsp kosher salt and 1 tsp ground ginger in a bowl and whisk them properly.
33. Grate 8 pieces cold unsalted butter and add it to the mixture using your fingers and incorporate the butter into the dough well. Make it perfect at the center of the mixture and add 1 cup of reduce cider and ½ cup of cold milk as well and use a spatula to mix the dough together.
34. Sprinkle the dough on a surface and have a few table spoons of flour on the surface for shaping the dough. Pat the dough into an even layer about an inch thick and sprinkle more flour. Fold and repeat the procedure again until the dough is less springy. Pat the dough into a 9x13 inch rectangular about ½ inches thick.
35. Cut the donut out of the dough using a floured donut cutter.

36. Transfer your donuts into a baking sheet and gather the scraps before patting the dough again and repeat this process until you have 18 donuts.
37. Preheat your air fryer and put it at 375 degrees Fahrenheit.
38. Melt the remaining butter in a medium pan and add granulated sugar and 1 tsp of ground cinnamon and whisk them together.
39. Depending on the size of the air fryer, you can bake a batch at a time until you have ready donuts. Serve the donuts warm once it is golden brown with warm cider for dipping.

NUTRITION: Calories 322 Fat 12.4g Carbs 49.1g Proteins 3.5g

Stuffing hushpuppies

Basic Recipe

Preparation Time: 10 minutes **Cooking Time:**
12 minutes **Servings:** 3 **INGREDIENTS:**

- Cooking trays
- 3 cups of cold stuffing
- 1 large egg

DIRECTIONS:

40. Place the egg in a large bowl and beat it. Add 3 cups of stuffing and stir until they are well combined.
41. Preheat your instant air fryer to 375 degrees Fahrenheit and set it to 12 minutes
42. Remove the cooking tray and spray it with a cooking spray before adding the hushpuppies into

    the racks. Spray on top of the hushpuppies as well. Cook for 6 minutes before flipping.
43. Once you are halfway flip the hushpuppies to allow for the other side to cook well. Repeat this with the remaining hushpuppies.
44. Serve with a sauce of your choice.

NUTRITION: Calories 237.4 Fat 16.6g Carbs 18.8g Proteins 3.2g

Fried Green Tomatoes

Basic Recipe

Preparation Time: 10 minutes **Cooking Time:**
15 minutes **Servings**: 6 **INGREDIENTS:**

- 1 cup bread crumbs
- 1/3 cup of versatile flour
- 1 cup yellow cornmeal
- 2 tomatoes cut into little slices
- ½ cup buttermilk
- 2 eggs, beaten gently

DIRECTIONS:

45. Season the slices of tomato with pepper and salt. Take 3 breeding meals. Keep flour in the very first, stir in eggs and buttermilk in the 2nd, and mix cornmeal and bread crumbs in the third. Dig up the pieces of tomato in your flour, shaking off any excess. Now dip the tomatoes in the egg mix, then in the bread crumb mix to coat both sides. Pre-heat your air fryer to 400 degrees F. Brush olive oil on the fryer basket. Keep the pieces of tomato in your fryer basket. Brush some olive oil on the tomato tops, cook for 10 minutes flip your tomatoes, brush olive oil and cook for another 5 minutes Take the tomatoes out. Keep in a rack lined with a paper towel. Serve.

NUTRITION: Calories 246 Carbs 40g Fat 6g Protein 8g

Air Fried Chicken Tenders

Basic Recipe

Preparation Time: 10 minutes **Cooking Time:**
10 minutes **Servings:** 4 **INGREDIENTS:**

- 1/8 cup flour
- Pepper and salt to taste
- Olive spray
- 1 egg white
- 12 oz, chicken breasts
- 1-¼ oz. panko bread crumbs

DIRECTIONS:

46. Trim off excess fat from your chicken breast. Cut into tenders. Season it with pepper and salt. Dip the tenders into flour and after that into egg whites and bread crumbs. Keep in the fryer basket. Apply olive spray and cook for 10 minutes at 350 degrees F. Serve.

NUTRITION: Calories 399 Carbs 18g Fat 11g Protein 57g

Parmesan Zucchini Chips

Basic Recipe

Preparation Time: 15 minutes **Cooking Time:** 10 minutes **Servings:** 4 **INGREDIENTS:**

- Salt to taste
- 3 medium zucchinis
- 1 cup grated Parmesan cheese

DIRECTIONS:

47. Preheat the oven in Air Fryer mode at 110 F for 2 to 3 minutes Use a mandolin slicer to very finely slice the zucchinis, season with salt, and coat well with the Parmesan cheese. In batches, arrange as lots of zucchini pieces as possible in a single layer on the cooking tray. When the device is ready, move the cooking tray onto the leading rack of the oven and close the oven. Set the timer to 7 minutes and press Start. Cook till the cheese melts while turning the midway. Transfer the chips to serving bowls to cool and make the remaining. Serve warm.

NUTRITION: Calories 107 Fat 6.99 g Carbs 3.73 g Protein 7.33 g

Cattle Ranch Garlic Pretzels

Basic Recipe

Preparation Time: 10 minutes **Cooking Time:** 15 minutes **Servings:** 4 **INGREDIENTS:**

- ½ tsp garlic powder
- 2 cups pretzels
- 1 ½ tsp ranch dressing mix
- 1 tbsp melted butter

DIRECTIONS:

48. Preheat the oven in Air Fryer mode at 270 F for 2 to 3 minutes. In a medium bowl, blend all the ingredients up until well-integrated, pour into the rotisserie basket and near to seal. Repair the basket onto the lever in the oven and close the oven. Set the timer to 15 minutes, press Start and cook until the pretzels are gently browner. After, open the oven, secure the basket utilizing the rotisserie lift and transfer the snack into serving bowls. Permit cooling and delight in.

NUTRITION: Calories 35 Fat 3.72 g Carbs 0.4 g Protein 0.12 g

Herby Sweet Potato Chips

Basic Recipe

Preparation Time: 10 minutes **Cooking Time:** 10 minutes **Servings:** 4 **INGREDIENTS:**

- 1 tsp dried mixed herbs
- 2 medium sweet potatoes, peeled
- 1 tbsp olive oil

DIRECTIONS:

49. Pre-heat the oven in Air Fry mode at 375 F for 2 to 3 minutes. On the other hand, utilize a mandolin slicer to thinly slice the sweet potatoes, transfer to a medium bowl and blend well with the herbs and olive oil till well coated. In batches, organize as numerous sweet potato pieces as possible in a single layer on the cooking tray. When the device is ready, slide the cooking tray onto the top rack of the oven and close the oven. Set the timer to 7 minutes and press Start. Cook till the sweet potatoes are crispy while turning midway. Transfer the chips to serving bowls when prepared and make the remaining in the same manner. Delight in.

NUTRITION: Calories 87 Fat 3.48 g Carbs 13.38 g Protein 1.03 g

Cumin Tortilla Chips with Guacamole

Basic Recipe

Preparation Time: 5 minutes **Cooking Time:** 15 minutes **Servings:** 4 **INGREDIENTS:**

- For the tortilla chips:
- 2 tablespoon olive oil
- 12 corn tortillas
- 1 tbsp paprika powder
- 1 tbsp cumin powder
- Salt and black pepper to taste
- For the guacamole:
- 1 little company tomato, sliced
- A pinch dried parsley
- 1 big avocado, pitted and peeled

DIRECTIONS:

50. Preheat the oven in Air Fry mode at 375 F for 2 to 3 minutes in a medium bowl, mix all the ingredients for the tortilla chips well and put the mix into the rotisserie basket. Close to seal. Fix the basket onto the lever in the oven and close the oven. Set the timer to 15 minutes, press Start and cook until the tortillas are golden brown.

51. After, open the oven, take out the basket using the rotisserie lift and transfer the chips to serving bowls.Meanwhile, as the chips cooked, in a little bowl, mash the avocados and blend with the tomato and parsley up until well combined.

52. Serve the tortilla chips with the guacamole. **NUTRITION:** Calories 159 Fat 14.74 g Carbs 7.82 g Protein 1.94 g

Oven-Dried Strawberries

Basic Recipe

Preparation Time: 10 minutes **Cooking Time:**
10 minutes **Servings:** 4 **INGREDIENTS:**

- 1-poundlarge strawberries

DIRECTIONS:

53. Pre-heat the air fryer in Dehydrate mode at 110 F for 2 to 3 minutes Use a mandolin slicer to thinly slice the strawberries. In batches, arrange a few of the strawberry pieces in a single layer on the cooking tray.
54. When the device is ready, move the cooking tray onto the top rack of the oven and close the oven
55. Set the timer to 7 minutes and press Start. Cook until the fruits are crispy.
56. Transfer the fruit chips to serving bowls when all set and make the remaining in the same manner. Delight in.

NUTRITION: Calories 36 Fat 0.34 g Carbs 8.71 g Protein 0.76 g

Chili Cheese Toasts

Basic Recipe

Preparation Time: 5 minutes **Cooking Time:**
10 minutes **Servings:** 4 **INGREDIENTS:**

- 1 tsp garlic powder
- 1 tsp red chili flakes
- 6 pieces sandwich bread
- 4 tablespoon butter
- 1 cup grated cheddar cheese
- 2 little fresh red chilies, deseeded and minced
- ½ tsp salt
- 1 tablespoon sliced fresh parsley

DIRECTIONS:

57. Pre-heat the oven in Broil mode at 375 F for 2 to 3 minutes Spread the butter on one side of each bread pieces and lay on a tidy, flat surface. Divide the cheddar cheese on top and followed with the remaining ingredients. Lay 3 pieces of the bread on the cooking tray, slide the tray onto the middle rack of the oven, and close the oven. Set the timer for 3 to 4 minutes and press Start. Cook till the cheese melts and is golden brown on top. Remove the first batch when ready and prepare the other three bread pieces. Slice them into triangle halves and serve immediately.

NUTRITION: Calories 105 Fat 11.53 g Carbs 0.68 g
Protein 0.29 g

Cheese Sticks

Basic Recipe

Preparation Time: 10 minutes **Cooking Time:** 10 minutes **Servings:** 6 **INGREDIENTS:**

- 1 teaspoon garlic powder
- 1 teaspoon of Italian spices
- ¼ teaspoon rosemary, ground
- 2 eggs
- 1 cheese sticks
- ¼ cup parmesan cheese, grated
- ¼ cup whole-wheat flour

DIRECTIONS:

58. Unwraps the cheese sticks. Keep aside. Beat the eggs into a bowl. Mix the cheese, flavorings, and flour in another bowl. Now roll the sticks in the egg and then into the batter. Coat well. Keep them in your air fryer basket. Cook for 7 minutes at 370 degrees F. Serve hot.

NUTRITION: Calories 76 Carbs 5g Fat 4g Protein 5g

Blended Veggie Chips

Basic Recipe

Preparation Time: 20 minutes **Cooking Time:**
10 minutes **Servings:** 4 **INGREDIENTS:**

- 1 big carrot
- 1 tsp salt
- 1 tsp Italian spices
- 1 zucchini
- 1 sweet potato peeled
- ½ tsp pepper
- 1 red beet, peeled
- A pinch cumin powders

DIRECTIONS:

59. Preheat the air fryer in Dehydrate mode at 110 F for 2 to 3 minutes
60. Utilize a mandolin slicer to thinly slice all the vegetables and transfer to a medium bowl. Season it with salt, Italian spices, and cumin powder. In batches, organize some of the veggies in a single layer on the cooking tray.
61. When the device is ready, move the cooking tray onto the top rack of the oven and close the oven then set the timer to 7 or 9 minutes and press Start.Cook up until the veggies are crispy. Transfer the vegetables to serving bowls when all set and make the staying in the same manner. Delight in.

NUTRITION: Calories 84 Fat 0.15 g Carbs 18.88 g Protein
2.25 g

Sweet Apple and Pear Chips

Basic Recipe

Preparation Time: 15 minutes **Cooking Time:**
10 minutes **Servings:** 4 **INGREDIENTS:**

- 6 pears, peeled
- 6 Honey crisp apples

DIRECTIONS:

62. Pre-heat the air fryer in Dehydrate mode at 110 F for 2 to 3 minutes. On the other hand, utilize a mandolin slicer to very finely slice the apples and pears. In batches, set up a few of the fruit slices in a single layer on the cooking tray.

63. When the device is ready, move the cooking tray onto the top rack of the oven and close the oven

64. Set the timer to 7 minutes and press Start. Cook till the fruits are crispy. Transfer the fruit chips to

serving bowls when all set and make the staying in the same manner. Take pleasure in.

NUTRITION: Calories 142 Fat 0.46 g Carbs 37.7g Protein 0.71g

Cocoa Banana Chips

Basic Recipe

Preparation Time: 5 minutes **Cooking Time:** 7
minutes **Servings:** 4 **INGREDIENTS:**

- ¼ tsp cocoa powder
- 5 large firm bananas, peeled
- A pinch of cinnamon powder

DIRECTIONS:

65. Preheat the air fryer in Dehydrate mode at 110 F for 2 to 3 minutes. On the other hand, utilize a mandolin slicer to very finely slice the bananas, and coat well with the cocoa powder and the cinnamon powder. In batches, organize as many banana pieces as possible in a single layer on the cooking tray.

66. When the device is ready, slide the cooking tray onto the top rack of the oven and close the oven set the timer to 7 minutes and press Start. Cook until the banana pieces are crispy. Transfer the chips to serving bowls when all set and make the remaining in the same manner. Take pleasure in.

NUTRITION: Calories 152 Fat 0.57 g Carbs 38.89 g
Protein 1.87 g

Coriander Roasted Chickpeas

Basic Recipe

Preparation Time: 10 minutes **Cooking Time:**
45minutes **Servings:** 2 **INGREDIENTS:**

- ¼ tsp garlic powder
- 1 (15 oz) can chickpeas, Dry-out pipes
- ¼ tsp ground coriander
- 1/8 tsp salt
- ¼ tsp chili pepper powder
- ¼ tsp curry powder
- ¼ tsp ground cumin
- ¼ tsp paprika
- Olive oil for spraying

DIRECTIONS:

67. Pre-heat the oven in Air Fryer mode at 375 F for 2 to 3 minutes in a medium bowl, mix the chickpeas with all the spices until well-integrated and pour into the rotisserie basket. Grease lightly with olive oil, shake the basket, and close the seal. Fix the basket onto the lever in the oven and close the oven. Set the timer to 35 or 45 minutes, press Start and cook up until the chickpeas are golden brown. After, open the oven, take out the basket utilizing the rotisserie lift and transfer the treat into serving bowls. Allow cooling and delight in.

NUTRITION: Calories 91 Fat 1.82 g Carbs 14.87 g Protein
4.61 g

LUNCH

Indian Cauliflower Curry

Basic Recipe

Preparation Time: 5 minutes **Cooking Time:** 15 minutes **Servings:** 4 **INGREDIENTS:**

- 240ml of vegetable stock
- 180ml of light coconut milk
- 1 ½ teaspoon of garam masala
- 1 teaspoon of mild curry powder
- 1 teaspoon of garlic puree
- 1/3 teaspoon of turmeric
- ¼ teaspoon of salt
- 350g of cauliflower florets
- 200g of sweet corn kernels
- 3 scallions

DIRECTIONS:

1. Preheat your Air Fryer to 375 degrees Fahrenheit.
2. Mix the vegetable stock, light coconut milk, garam masala, mild curry powder, garlic puree, turmeric and salt in a large bowl.
3. Add in the cauliflower, sweet corn and the scallions. Mix them in until coated.
4. Place in a dish and put inside the Air Fryer, cook at 375 degrees Fahrenheit for 12 to 15 minutes

NUTRITION: Calories 166 Fat 4g Carbs 29g Protein 4g

Thai Green Curry Noodles

Intermediate Recipe

Preparation Time: 1 hour and 15 minutes
Cooking Time: 20 minutes **Servings:** 6
INGREDIENTS:

- 1kg of shirataki noodles
- 6 tablespoons of soy sauce
- 1 ½ tablespoon of fish sauce
- 1 teaspoon of sesame oil
- ½ teaspoon garlic powder
- 350g of tofu
- 150g of snow peas
- 1 red pepper
  - 1 green pepper
  - 100g of mushrooms
  - 150g of water chestnuts
  - 1 teaspoon of coriander paste
  - 3 tablespoons of lime juice
  - 2 teaspoons of lemongrass paste
  - 4 tablespoons of rice wine vinegar
  - 350g of napa cabbage
  - 2 medium carrots
  - 4 green onions
  - 6 tablespoons of thai green curry paste

DIRECTIONS

1. Firstly, to prepare the vegetables make sure both peppers, mushrooms water chestnuts are sliced thinly. The carrots and cabbage need to be shredded and lastly, the green onions chopped finely. Set aside for later.
2. Place the noodles in a large bowl with 500 ml of boiling water, stirring in 1 tablespoon of the soy sauce. Set aside.
3. Mix 3 tablespoons of the soy sauce, fish sauce, sesame oil and garlic powder together to make a marinade.
4. Cut the tofu into bite-size cubes and put into the marinade, making sure to mix together. Set aside.
5. In a bowl to make the stir-fry veg, mix the snow peas, peppers,

55

mushrooms and water chestnuts. Set aside.

6. To make the dressing, mix the coriander paste, lime juice, lemongrass paste and 4 tablespoons of the Thai green curry paste and 2 tablespoons of the rice vinegar. Set aside.

7. To make the veg base, mix the shredded cabbage, shredded carrots and the chopped green onion. Set aside.

8. Set the Air Fryer temperature to 360 degrees Fahrenheit and spray the basket with cooking oil.

9. Remove the tofu from the marinade and place into the Air Fryer basket, cook for 12 to 13 minutes Make sure to turn halfway through the cooking process. Once done, set aside with a plate on top to keep them warm.

10. Mix the leftover marinade, 2 tablespoons of rice vinegar, 2 tablespoons of soy sauce, 2 tablespoons of the Thai green curry paste, place into a bowl suitable for the Air Fryer, mix in the stir-fry veg and spray with the cooking oil. Cook for 5 minutes

11. Dry out the noodles.

12. In a large bowl, put in: the noodles, the dressing, the tofu cubes, the stir-fry veg and the veg base. Toss with tongs to mix everything together.

NUTRITION: Calories 183 Fat 6.1g Carbs 22.7g Protein 9.9g

Italian Salmon

Basic Recipe

Preparation Time: 5 minutes **Cooking Time:**
10 minutes **Servings:** 2

INGREDIENTS:

- 340g of salmon fillets
- 1 ½ tablespoons of butter
- 2 garlic cloves
- 1 tablespoon of lemon juice
- 2 teaspoons of brown sugar
- 2 teaspoons of parsley
- ½ teaspoon of dried italian seasoning
- ½ teaspoon of pepper
- ½ teaspoon of salt

DIRECTIONS

13. To prep, mince the garlic and finely chop the parsley.
14. Melt the butter and mix in the garlic, lemon juice, brown sugar, parsley and Italian seasoning.
15. Coat the salmon fillets in the butter mixture.
16. Next, season the salmon fillets with salt and pepper.
17. Place the salmon fillets in the Air Fryer and cook at 390 degrees Fahrenheit for 7 to 8 minutes Turn halfway through cooking. The internal temperature should be at least 145 degrees Fahrenheit.

NUTRITION: Calories 332 Fat 19g Carbs 4g Protein 34g

Mexican Taco Salad Bowl

Basic Recipe

Preparation Time: 2 minutes **Cooking Time:**
10 minutes **Servings:** 2 **INGREDIENTS:**

- 1 Burrito Sized Flour Tortilla
- Cooking Spray

DIRECTIONS:

1. Spray both sides of the tortilla with cooking spray.
2. Fold a piece of foil, which is double the size of the tortilla and place it over the tortilla wrap.
3. Place into the Air Fryer and put a bowl just slightly smaller inside, this will help to weigh it down.
4. Cook the tortilla at 400 degrees Fahrenheit for 5 minutes
5. Remove the bowl and then Air Fry for a further 2 minutes
6. Fill the burrito bowl with salad ingredients of your choice.

NUTRITION: Calories 220 Fat 20g Carbs 84g Protein 21g

Italian Ratatouille

Intermediate Recipe Preparation Time: 25 minutes **Cooking Time:** 25 minutes **Servings:** 4

INGREDIENTS:

- ½ Small eggplants
- 1 zucchini
- 1 medium tomato
- ½ large yellow bell pepper
- ½ large red bell peppers
- ½ onions
- 1 cayenne pepper
- 5 basil sprigs
- 2 oregano sprigs
- 1 garlic clove
- ½ teaspoon of salt
- ½ teaspoon of pepper
- 1 tablespoon of olive oil
- 1 tablespoon of white wine
- 1 teaspoon of vinegar

DIRECTIONS:

1. Preheat your Air Fryer to 400 degrees Fahrenheit.
2. Next, cut the zucchini, tomato, both bell peppers, onion, cayenne pepper into cubes. Then steam and chop the basil and oregano leaves.
3. Mix the eggplant, zucchini, tomato, bell peppers, onions, cayenne pepper, basil, oregano, garlic, salt and pepper in a bowl. Drizzle with the mixture in oil, wine and vinegar.
4. Find a baking dish that fits inside of your Air Fryer and pour the vegetable mixture into the bowl.
5. Put the baking dish into the Air Fryer and cook for 8 minutes Once the 8 minutes are up, stir and then cook for a further 8 minutes Stir again and keep cooking until the vegetables become tender, make sure to stir every 5 minutes for another 10 minutes

NUTRITION: Calories 79 Calories Fat 3.8g Carbs 10.2g Protein 2.1g

Chinese Crispy Vegetables

Basic Recipe

Preparation Time: 10 minutes **Cooking Time:** 15 minutes **Servings:** 2 **INGREDIENTS:**

- 260g of mixed vegetables e.g. Bell peppers, cauliflower, mushrooms, zucchini, baby corn
- 20g of corn-starch
- 20g of all-purpose flour
- ½ teaspoon of garlic powder
- ½ teaspoon of red chili powder
- ½ teaspoon of black pepper powder
- 1 teaspoon of salt
- 1 teaspoon of olive oil
- 2 tablespoons of soy sauce
- 1 tablespoon of chili sauce
- 1 tablespoon of ketchup
- 1 tablespoon of vinegar
- 1 teaspoon of brown sugar
- 1 tablespoon of sesame oil
- 1 teaspoon of sesame seeds

DIRECTIONS:

1. Cut the cauliflower in small florets. Cube the bell peppers, cut the mushrooms in half. Cut the carrots and zucchini in circles.
2. To make the batter, mix the all-purpose flour, corn- starch, garlic powder, bell pepper powder, red chili powder and the salt together.
3. Add a teaspoon of oil to the batter, mix until not lumpy.
4. Add the vegetables to the batter and make sure they are evenly coated.
5. Preheat your Air Fryer to 350 degrees Fahrenheit.
6. Add the vegetables to the Air Fryer basket and cook for 10 minutes
7. In a saucepan, add a tablespoon of oil, finely chopped garlic, heat until it gives an aroma. Then add the soy sauce, chili sauce, tomato ketchup, vinegar, brown sugar and the black pepper powder.
8. Cook the sauce for a minute then add the Air Fried vegetables and mix well. Make sure the vegetables are evenly coated.

9. Sprinkle the sesame seeds and sesame oil over the vegetables.

NUTRITION: Calories 236 Fat 10.5g Carbs 32.2g Protein 4.6g

Chinese Salt and Pepper Tofu

Basic Recipe

Preparation Time: 20 minutes **Cooking Time:** 15 minutes **Servings:** 2 **INGREDIENTS:**

- 450g of tofu
- ¾ teaspoon of sea salt
- ¾ teaspoon of ground white pepper
- 2 pinches of chinese spice powder
- 1 teaspoon of sugar
- 3 tablespoons of canola
- 1 tablespoon of corn-starch
- 3 ½ tablespoons of rice flour
- 3 garlic cloves
- 1 serrano chile
- 2 large scallions

DIRECTIONS:

1. Preheat your Air Fryer to 375 degrees Fahrenheit.
2. Cut tofu into bite-size pieces and mix with ¼ teaspoon of the salt. Put on paper towels and let the moisture Dry out.
3. In a bowl, stir together ¼ teaspoon of salt, 1/8 teaspoon of pepper, Chinese spice and the sugar. Put half of the mixture into a bowl and add the corn-starch and rice flour.
4. Coat the tofu in 1 tablespoon of the canola oil and then cover in the seasoned starch and flour mixture.
5. Put the tofu into the Air Fryer basket and cook at 375 degrees Fahrenheit for 15 minutes Make sure to toss halfway through the cooking process.
6. Whilst cooking, in wok mix 2 tablespoons canola oil, garlic, chili and scallions. Cook for about half a minute until fragrant.
7. Add the tofu to the wok and then sprinkle in the remaining salt, pepper, Chinese spice and sugar mixture. Cook for 1 to 2 minutes, making sure to stir continuously.

NUTRITION: Calories 466 Fat 30.9g Carbs 31.6g Protein 21.5g

Indian Almond Crusted Fried Masala Fish

Intermediate Recipe Preparation Time: 30
minutes **Cooking Time:** 20 minutes **Servings:** 4
INGREDIENTS:

- 900g of fish fillet
- 4 tablespoons of extra virgin olive oil
- ¾ teaspoon of turmeric
- 1 teaspoon of cayenne pepper
- 1 teaspoon of salt
- 1 tablespoon of fenugreek leaves
- 1 ½ teaspoons of ground cumin
- 2 teaspoons of amchoor powder
- 2 tablespoons of ground almonds

DIRECTIONS:

1. In a bowl, combine the oil, turmeric, cayenne, salt, fenugreek leaves, cumin and amchoor powder. After combining mix in the ground almonds, put the fish into a bowl and pour the mixture over the fish. Mix around to evenly cover the fish.
2. Put the fish into the Air Fryer basket and cook for 450 degrees Fahrenheit for 10 minutes Turnover and then cook for a further 10 minutes

NUTRITION: Calories 675 Calories Fat 43.6g Carbs 41.7g Protein 34.5g

Greek Chicken

Basic Recipe

Preparation Time: 10 minutes **Cooking Time:** 15 minutes **Servings:** 4 **INGREDIENTS:**

- 2 tablespoons olive oil
- Juice from 1 lemon
- 1 teaspoon oregano, dried
- 3 garlic cloves, minced
- 1-pound chicken thighs
- Salt and black pepper to the taste
- ½ pound asparagus, trimmed
- 1 zucchini, roughly chopped
- 1 lemon sliced

DIRECTIONS:

1. In a heat proof dish that fits your air fryer, mix chicken pieces with oil, lemon juice, oregano, garlic, salt, pepper, asparagus, zucchini and lemon slices, toss, introduce in preheated air fryer and cook at 380 degrees F for 15 minutes Divide everything on plates and serve. Enjoy!

NUTRITION: Calories 300 Fat 8 Carbs 20 Protein 18

Duck Breasts with Red Wine and Orange Sauce

Basic Recipe

Preparation Time: 10 minutes **Cooking Time:** 35 minutes **Servings:** 4 **INGREDIENTS:**

- ½ cup honey
- 2 cups orange juice
- 4 cups red wine
- 2 tablespoons sherry vinegar
- 2 cups chicken stock
- 2 teaspoons pumpkin pie spice
- 2 tablespoons butter
- 2 duck breasts, skin on and halved
- 2 tablespoons olive oil
- salt and black pepper to the taste

DIRECTIONS:

1. Heat up a pan with the orange juice over medium heat, add honey, stir well and cook for 10 minutes Add wine, vinegar, stock, pie spice and butter, stir well, cook for 10 minutes more and take off heat. Season duck breasts with salt and pepper, rub with olive oil, place in preheated air fryer at 370 degrees F and cook for 7 minutes on each side. Divide duck breasts on plates, Drizzle with wine and orange juice all over and serve right away. Enjoy!

NUTRITION: Calories 300 Fat 8 Carbs 24 Protein 11

Easy Duck Breasts

Basic Recipe

Preparation Time: 10 minutes **Cooking Time:**
15 minutes **Servings:** 4 **INGREDIENTS:**

- 4 duck breasts, skinless and boneless
- 4 garlic heads, peeled, tops cut off and quartered
- 2 tablespoons lemon juice
- Salt and black pepper to the taste
- ½ teaspoon lemon pepper
- 1 and ½ tablespoon olive oil

DIRECTIONS:

1. In a bowl, mix duck breasts with garlic, lemon juice, salt, pepper, lemon pepper and olive oil and toss everything.
2. Transfer duck and garlic to your air fryer and cook at 350 degrees F for 15 minutes Divide duck breasts and garlic on plates and serve. Enjoy!

NUTRITION: Calories 200 Fat 7 Carbs 11 Protein 17

Duck Breast with Fig Sauce

Basic Recipe

Preparation Time: 10 minutes **Cooking Time:**
20 minutes **Servings:** 4 **INGREDIENTS:**

- 2 duck breasts, skin on, halved
- 1 tablespoon olive oil
- ½ teaspoon thyme, chopped
- ½ teaspoon garlic powder
- ¼ teaspoon sweet paprika
- Salt and black pepper to the taste
- 1 cup beef stock
- 3 tablespoons butter, melted
- 1 shallot, chopped
- ½ cup port wine
- 4 tablespoons fig preserves
- 1 tablespoon white flour

DIRECTIONS:

1. Season duck breasts with salt and pepper, Drizzle with half of the melted butter, rub well, put in your air fryer's basket and cook at 350 degrees F for 5 minutes on each side. Meanwhile, heat up a pan with the olive oil and the rest of the butter over medium high heat, add shallot, stir and cook for 2 minutes Add thyme, garlic powder, paprika, stock, salt, pepper, wine and figs, stir and cook for 7-8 minutes Add flour, stir well, cook until sauce thickens a bit and take off heat. Divide duck breasts on plates, Drizzle with figs sauce all over and serve. Enjoy!

NUTRITION: Calories 246 Fat 12 Carbs 22 Protein 3

Duck Breasts and Raspberry Sauce

Basic Recipe

Preparation Time: 10 minutes **Cooking Time:** 15 minutes **Servings:** 4 **INGREDIENTS:**

- 2 duck breasts, skin on and scored
- Salt and black pepper to the taste
- Cooking spray
- ½ teaspoon cinnamon powder
- ½ cup raspberries
- 1 tablespoon of sugar
- 1 teaspoon red wine vinegar
- ½ cup water

DIRECTIONS:

1. Season duck breasts with salt and pepper, spray them with cooking spray, put in preheated air fryer skin side down and cook at 350 degrees F for 10 minutes Heat up a pan with the water over medium heat, add raspberries, cinnamon, sugar and wine, stir, bring to a simmer, transfer to your blender, puree and return to pan. Add air fryer duck breasts to pan as well, toss to coat, divide among plates and serve right away. Enjoy!

NUTRITION: Calories 456 Fat 22 Carbs 14 Protein 45

Chicken Breasts with Passion Fruit Sauce

Intermediate Recipe Preparation Time: 10 minutes
Cooking Time: 10 minutes **Servings:** 4
INGREDIENTS:

- 4 chicken breasts
- Salt and black pepper to the taste
- 4 passion fruits, halved, deseeded and pulp reserved
- 1 tablespoon whiskey
- 2-star anise
- 2 ounces maple syrup
- 1 bunch chives, chopped

DIRECTIONS:

1. Heat up a pan with the passion fruit pulp over medium heat, add whiskey, star anise, maple syrup and chives, stir well, simmer for 5- 6 minutes and take off heat. Season chicken with salt and pepper, put in preheated air fryer and cook at 360 degrees F for 10 minutes, flipping halfway. Divide chicken on plates, heat up the sauce a bit, Drizzle with it over chicken and serve. Enjoy!

NUTRITION: Calories 374 Fat 8 Carbs 34 Protein 37

Duck and Cherries

Basic Recipe

Preparation Time: 10 minutes **Cooking Time:**
20 minutes **Servings:** 4 **INGREDIENTS:**

- ½ cup sugar
- ¼ cup honey
- 1/3 cup balsamic vinegar
- 1 teaspoon garlic, minced
- 1 tablespoon ginger, grated
- 1 teaspoon cumin, ground
- ½ teaspoon clove, ground
- ½ teaspoon cinnamon powder
- 4 sage leaves, chopped
- 1 jalapeno, chopped
- 2 cups rhubarb, sliced
- ½ cup yellow onion, chopped
- 2 cups cherries, pitted
- 4 duck breasts, boneless, skin on and scored
- Salt and black pepper to the taste

DIRECTIONS:

1. Season duck breast with salt and pepper, put in your air fryer and cook at 350 degrees F for 5 minutes on each side.
2. Meanwhile, heat up a pan over medium heat, add sugar, honey, vinegar, garlic, ginger, cumin, clove, cinnamon, sage, jalapeno, rhubarb, onion and cherries, stir, bring to a simmer and cook for 10 minutes
3. Add duck breasts, toss well, divide everything on plates and serve. Enjoy!

NUTRITION: Calories 456 Fat 13 Carbs 64 Protein 31

Duck and Tea Sauce

Basic Recipe

Preparation Time: 10 minutes **Cooking Time:**
20 minutes **Servings:** 4 **INGREDIENTS:**

- 2 duck breast halves, boneless

    - 2 and ¼ cup chicken stock
    - ¾ cup shallot, chopped
    - 1 and ½ cup orange juice
    - Salt and black pepper to the taste
    - 3 teaspoons earl gray tea leaves
    - 3 tablespoons butter, melted
    - 1 tablespoon honey

DIRECTIONS:

1. Season duck breast halves with salt and pepper, put in preheated air fryer and cook at 360 degrees F for
10 minutes Meanwhile, heat up a pan with the butter over medium heat, add shallot, stir and cook for 2-3 minutes Add stock, stir and cook for another minute. Add orange juice, tea leaves and honey, stir, cook for 2-3 minutes more and strain into a bowl. Divide duck on plates, Drizzle with tea sauce all over and serve. Enjoy!

NUTRITION: Calories 228 Fat 11 Carbs 20 Protein 12

Marinated Duck Breasts

Intermediate Recipe Preparation Time: 1 day **Cooking Time:** 20 minutes **Servings:** 2

INGREDIENTS:

- 2 duck breasts
- 1 cup white wine
- ¼ cup soy sauce
- 2 garlic cloves, minced
- 6 tarragon springs
- Salt and black pepper to the taste
- 1 tablespoon butter
- ¼ cup sherry wine

DIRECTIONS:

1. In a bowl, mix duck breasts with white wine, soy sauce, garlic, tarragon, salt and pepper, toss well and keep in the fridge for 1 day. Transfer duck breasts to your preheated air fryer at 350 degrees F and cook for 10 minutes, flipping halfway.
2. Meanwhile, pour the marinade in a pan, heat up over medium heat, add butter and sherry, stir, bring to a simmer, cook for 5 minutes and take off heat. Divide duck breasts on plates, Drizzle with sauce all over and serve. Enjoy!

NUTRITION: Calories 475 Fat 12 Carbs 10 Protein 48

Chicken and Radish Mix

Basic Recipe

Preparation Time: 10 minutes **Cooking Time:** 30 minutes **Servings:** 4 **INGREDIENTS:**

- 4 chicken things, bone-in
- Salt and black pepper to the taste
- 1 tablespoon olive oil
- 1 cup chicken stock
- 6 radishes, halved
- 1 teaspoon sugar
- 3 carrots cut into thin sticks
- 2 tablespoon chives, chopped

DIRECTIONS:

1. Heat up a pan that fits your air fryer over medium heat, add stock, carrots, sugar and radishes, stir gently, reduce heat to medium, cover pot partly and simmer for 20 minutes Rub chicken with olive oil, season with salt and pepper, put in your air fryer and cook at 350 degrees F for 4 minutes.
2. Add chicken to radish mix, toss, introduce everything in your air fryer, cook for 4 minutes more, divide among plates and serve. Enjoy!

NUTRITION: Calories 237 Fat 10 Carbs 19 Protein 29

Chicken Breasts and BBQ Chili Sauce

Basic Recipe

Preparation Time: 10 minutes **Cooking Time:**
20 minutes **Servings:** 6 **INGREDIENTS:**

- 2 cups chili sauce
- 2 cups ketchup
- 1 cup pear jelly
- ¼ cup honey
- ½ teaspoon liquid smoke
- 1 teaspoon chili powder
- 1 teaspoon mustard powder
- 1 teaspoon sweet paprika
- Salt and black pepper to the taste
- 1 teaspoon garlic powder
- 6 chicken breasts, skinless and boneless

DIRECTIONS:

1. Season chicken breasts with salt and pepper, put in preheated air fryer and cook at 350 degrees F for 10 minutes Meanwhile, heat up a pan with the chili sauce over medium heat, add ketchup, pear jelly, honey, liquid smoke, chili powder, mustard powder, sweet paprika, salt, pepper and the garlic powder, stir, bring to a simmer and cook for 10 minutes Add air fried chicken breasts, toss well, divide among plates and serve. Enjoy!

NUTRITION: Calories 473 Fat 13 Carbs 39 Protein 33

Duck Breasts and Mango Mix

Intermediate Recipe Preparation Time: 1 hour **Cooking Time:** 20 minutes **Servings:** 4

INGREDIENTS:

- 4 duck breasts
- 1 and ½ tablespoons lemongrass, chopped
- 3 tablespoons lemon juice
- 2 tablespoons olive oil
- Salt and black pepper to the taste
- 3 garlic cloves, minced
- For the mango mix:

- 1 mango, peeled and chopped
- 1 tablespoon coriander, chopped
- 1 red onion, chopped
- 1 tablespoon sweet chili sauce
- 1 and ½ tablespoon lemon juice
- 1 teaspoon ginger, grated
- ¾ teaspoon sugar

DIRECTIONS:

1. In a bowl, mix duck breasts with salt, pepper, lemongrass, 3 tablespoons lemon juice, olive oil and garlic, toss well, keep in the fridge for 1 hour, transfer to your air fryer and cook at 360 degrees F for 10 minutes, flipping once. Meanwhile, in a bowl, mix mango with coriander, onion, chili sauce, lemon juice, ginger and sugar and toss well. Divide duck on plates, add mango mix on the side and serve. Enjoy!

NUTRITION: Calories 465 Fat 11 Carbs 29 Protein 38

Quick Creamy Chicken Casserole

Basic Recipe

Preparation Time: 10 minutes **Cooking Time:** 15 minutes **Servings:** 4 **INGREDIENTS:**

- 10 ounces spinach, chopped
- 4 tablespoons butter
- 3 tablespoons flour
- 1 and ½ cups milk
- ½ cup parmesan, grated
- ½ cup heavy cream
- Salt and black pepper to the taste
- 2 cup chicken breasts, skinless, boneless and cubed
- 1 cup bread crumbs

DIRECTIONS:

1. Heat up a pan with the butter over medium heat,   add flour and stir well. Add milk, heavy cream and parmesan, stir well, cook for 1-2 minutes more and take off heat. In a pan that fits your air fryer, spread chicken and spinach. Add salt and pepper and toss. Add cream mix and spread, sprinkle bread crumbs on top, introduce in your air fryer and cook at 350 for 12 minutes Divide chicken and spinach mix on plates and serve. Enjoy!

NUTRITION: Calories 321 Fat 9 Carbs 22 Protein 17

Chicken and Peaches

Basic Recipe

Preparation Time: 10 minutes **Cooking Time:** 30 minutes **Servings:** 6 **INGREDIENTS:**

- 1 whole chicken, cut into medium pieces
- ¾ cup water
- 1/3 cup honey
- Salt and black pepper to the taste
- ¼ cup olive oil
- 4 peaches, halved

DIRECTIONS:

1. Put the water in a pot, bring to a simmer over medium heat, add honey, whisk really well and leave aside. Rub chicken pieces with the oil, season with salt and pepper, place in your air fryer's basket and cook at 350 degrees F for 10 minutes Brush chicken with some of the honey mix, cook for 6 minutes more, flip again, brush one more time with the honey mix and cook for 7 minutes more. Divide chicken pieces on plates and keep warm. Brush peaches with what's left of the honey marinade, place them in your air fryer and cook them for 3 minutes Divide among plates next to chicken pieces and serve. Enjoy!

NUTRITION: Calories 430 Fat 14 Carbs 15 Protein 20

Tea Glazed Chicken

Basic Recipe

Preparation Time: 10 minutes **Cooking Time:**
30 minutes **Servings:** 6 **INGREDIENTS:**

- ½ cup apricot preserves
- ½ cup pineapple preserves
- 6 chicken legs
- 1 cup hot water
- 6 black tea bags
- 1 tablespoon soy sauce
- 1 onion, chopped
- ¼ teaspoon red pepper flakes
- 1 tablespoon olive oil
- Salt and black pepper to the taste
- 6 chicken legs

DIRECTIONS:

1. Put the hot water in a bowl, add tea bags, leave aside covered for 10 minutes, discard bags at the end and transfer tea to another bowl. Add soy sauce, pepper flakes, apricot and pineapple preserves, whisk really well and take off heat.
2. Season chicken with salt and pepper, rub with oil, put in your air fryer and cook at 350 degrees F for 5 minutes Spread onion on the bottom of a baking dish that fits your air fryer, add chicken pieces, Drizzle with the tea glaze on top, introduce in your air fryer and cook at 320 degrees F for 25 minutes Divide everything on plates and serve. Enjoy!

NUTRITION: Calories 298 Fat 14 Carbs 14 Protein 30

Ratatouille

Basic Recipe

Preparation Time: 10 minutes **Cooking Time:** 20 minutes **Servings:** 4 **INGREDIENTS:**

- 4 Roma tomatoes, seeded and chopped
- 3 garlic cloves, sliced
- 1 baby eggplant, peeled and chopped
  - 1 red bell pepper, chopped
  - 1 yellow bell pepper, chopped
  - 1 small onion, chopped
  - 1 teaspoon Italian seasoning
  - 1 teaspoon olive oil

DIRECTIONS:

1. In a medium metal bowl, gently combine the tomatoes, garlic, eggplant, red and yellow bell peppers, onion, Italian seasoning, and olive oil. Place the bowl in the air fryer. Roast for 12 to 16 minutes, stirring once, until the vegetables are tender. Serve warm or cold.

NUTRITION: Calories 69 Fat 2g Protein 2g Carbs 11g

Vegetable Egg Rolls

Basic Recipe

Preparation Time: 15 minutes **Cooking Time:** 10 minutes **Servings:** 4 **INGREDIENTS:**

- ½ cup chopped yellow summer squash
- ⅓ cup grated carrot
- ½ cup chopped red bell pepper
- 2 scallions, white and green parts, chopped
- 1 teaspoon low-sodium soy sauce
- 4 egg roll wrappers (see Tip)
- 1 tablespoon cornstarch
- 1 egg, beaten

DIRECTIONS:

1. In a medium bowl, mix the yellow squash, carrot, red bell pepper, scallions, and soy sauce.
2. Place the egg roll wrappers on a work surface. Top each with about 3 tablespoons of the vegetable mixture.
3. In a small bowl, thoroughly mix the cornstarch and egg. Brush some egg mixture on the edges of each wrapper. Roll up the wrappers, folding over the sides so the filling is contained. Brush the egg mixture on the outside of each egg roll.
4. Air-fry it for 7 to 10 minutes or until brown and crunchy then serve immediately.

NUTRITION: Calories 130 Fat 2g Protein 6g Carbs 23g

Grilled Cheese and Greens Sandwiches

Basic Recipe

Preparation Time: 15 minutes **Cooking Time:**
10 minutes **Servings:** 4 **INGREDIENTS:**

- 1½ cups chopped mixed greens (kale, chard, collards; see Tip)
- 2 garlic cloves, thinly sliced
- 2 teaspoons olive oil
- 2 slices low-sodium low-fat Swiss cheese
- 4 slices low-sodium whole-wheat bread
- Olive oil spray, for coating the sandwiches

DIRECTIONS:

1. In a 6-by-2-inch pan, mix the greens, garlic, and olive oil. Cook in the air fryer for 4 to 5 minutes, stirring once, until the vegetables are tender. Dry out, if necessary.
2. Make 2 sandwiches, dividing half of the greens and 1 slice of Swiss cheese between 2 slices of bread. Lightly spray the outsides of the sandwiches with olive oil spray.
3. Grill the sandwiches in the air fryer for 6 to 8 minutes, turning with tongs halfway through, until the bread is toasted and the cheese melts.
4. Cut each sandwich in half to serve.

NUTRITION: Calories 176 Fat 6g Protein 10g Carbs 24g

Veggie Tuna Melts

Basic Recipe

Preparation Time: 15 minutes **Cooking Time:**
10 minutes **Servings:** 4 **INGREDIENTS:**

- 2 low-sodium whole-wheat English muffins split
- 1 (6-ounce) can chunk light low-sodium tuna, Dry outed
- 1 cup shredded carrot
- ⅓ cup chopped mushrooms
- 2 scallions, white and green parts, sliced
- ⅓ cup nonfat Greek yogurt
- 2 tablespoons low-sodium stone-ground mustard
- 2 slices low-sodium low-fat Swiss cheese, halved

DIRECTIONS:

1. Place the English muffin halves in the air fryer basket. Grill for 3 to 4 minutes, or until crisp. Remove from the basket and set aside.
2. In a medium bowl, thoroughly mix the tuna, carrot, mushrooms, scallions, yogurt, and mustard. Top each half of the muffins with one-fourth of the tuna mixture and a half slice of Swiss cheese.
3. Grill in the air fryer for 4 to 7 minutes, or until the tuna mixture is hot and the cheese melts and starts to brown. Serve immediately.

NUTRITION: Calories 191 Fat 4g Protein 23g Carbs 16g

California Melts

Basic Recipe

Preparation Time: 10 minutes **Cooking Time:**
5 minutes **Servings:** 4 **INGREDIENTS:**

- 2 low-sodium whole-wheat English muffins split
- 2 tablespoons nonfat Greek yogurt
- 8 fresh baby spinach leaves
- 1 ripe tomato, cut into 4 slices
- ½ ripe avocados, peeled, pitted, and sliced lengthwise (see Tip)
- 8 fresh basil leaves
- 4 tablespoons crumbled fat-free low-sodium feta cheese, divided

DIRECTIONS:

1. Put the English muffin halves into the air fryer. Toast for 2 minutes, or until light golden brown. Transfer to a work surface.
2. Spread each muffin half with 1½ teaspoons of yogurt.
3. Top each muffin half with 2 spinach leaves, 1 tomato slice, one-fourth of the avocado, and 2 basil leaves. Sprinkle each with 1 tablespoon of feta cheese. Toast the sandwiches in the air fryer for 3 to 4 minutes, or until the cheese softens and the sandwich is hot. Serve immediately.

NUTRITION: Calories 110 Fat 3g Protein 8g Carbs 13g

Vegetable Pita Sandwiches

Basic Recipe

Preparation Time: 10 minutes **Cooking Time:** 20 minutes **Servings:** 4 **INGREDIENTS:**

- 1 baby eggplant peeled and chopped (see Tip)
- 1 red bell pepper, sliced
- ½ cup diced red onion
- ½ cup shredded carrot
- 1 teaspoon olive oil
- ⅓ cup low-fat Greek yogurt
- ½ teaspoon dried tarragon
- 2 low-sodium whole-wheat pita breads, halved crosswise

DIRECTIONS:

4. In a 6-by-2-inch pan, stir together the eggplant, red bell pepper, red onion, carrot, and olive oil. Put the vegetable mixture into the air fryer basket and roast for 7 to 9 minutes, stirring once, until the vegetables are tender. Dry out if necessary.
5. In a small bowl, thoroughly mix the yogurt and tarragon until well combined.
6. Stir the yogurt mixture into the vegetables. Stuff one-fourth of this mixture into each pita pocket.
7. Place the sandwiches in the air fryer and cook for 2 to 3 minutes, or until the bread is toasted. Serve immediately.

NUTRITION: Calories 176 Fat 4g Protein 7g Carbs 27g

Falafel

Basic Recipe

Preparation Time: 10 minutes **Cooking Time:** 20 minutes **Servings:** 4 **INGREDIENTS:**

- 1 (16-ounce) can no-salt-added chickpeas rinsed and Dry outed
- ⅓ cup whole-wheat pastry flour
- ⅓ cup minced red onion
- 2 garlic cloves, minced
- 2 tablespoons minced fresh cilantro
- 1 tablespoon olive oil
- ½ teaspoon ground cumin
- ¼ teaspoon cayenne pepper

DIRECTIONS:

8. In a medium bowl, mash the chickpeas with a potato masher until mostly smooth.
9. Stir in the pastry flour, red onion, garlic, cilantro, olive oil, cumin, and cayenne until well mixed. Firm the chickpea mixture into 12 balls. Air-fry the falafel balls, in batches, for 11 to 13 minutes, or until the falafel are firm and light golden brown. Serve.

NUTRITION: Calories 172 Fat 5g Protein 7g Carbs 25g

Stuffed Tomatoes

Basic Recipe

Preparation Time: 5 minutes **Cooking Time:**
20 minutes **Servings:** 4 **INGREDIENTS:**

- 4 medium beefsteak tomatoes, rinsed and patted dry
- 1 medium onion, chopped
- ½ cup grated carrot
- 1 garlic clove, minced
- 2 teaspoons olive oil
- 2 cups fresh baby spinach
- ¼ cup crumbled low-sodium feta cheese
- ½ teaspoon dried basil

DIRECTIONS:

10. Cut about ½ inch off the top of each tomato. Gently hollow them out (see Tip), leaving a wall about ½ inch thick. Dry out the tomatoes, upside down, on paper towels while you prepare the filling.
11. In a 6-by-2-inch pan, mix the onion, carrot, garlic, and olive oil. Bake it for 4 to 6 minutes, or until the vegetables are crisp-tender.
12. Stir in the spinach, feta cheese, and basil.
13. Fill each tomato with one-fourth of the vegetable mixture. Bake the tomatoes in the air fryer basket for 12 to 14 minutes, or until hot and tender.
14. Serve immediately.

NUTRITION: Calories 79 Fat 3g Protein 3g Carbs 9g

Loaded Mini Potatoes

Basic Recipe

Preparation Time: 5 minutes **Cooking Time:**
25 minutes **Servings:** 2 **INGREDIENTS:**

- 24 small new potatoes, or creamer potatoes, rinsed, scrubbed, and patted dry
- 1 teaspoon olive oil
- ½ cup low-fat Greek yogurt
- 1 tablespoon low-sodium stone-ground mustard (see Tip)
- ½ teaspoon dried basil
- 3 Roma tomatoes, seeded and chopped
- 2 scallions, white and green parts, chopped
- 2 tablespoons chopped fresh chives

DIRECTIONS:

1. In a large bowl, toss the potatoes with the olive oil. Transfer to the air fryer basket. Roast for 20 to 25

   minutes, shaking the basket once, until the potatoes are crisp on the outside and tender within. Meanwhile, in a small bowl, stir together the yogurt, mustard, and basil.
2. Place the potatoes on a serving platter and carefully smash each one slightly with the bottom of a drinking glass. Top the potatoes with the yogurt mixture. Sprinkle with the tomatoes, scallions, and chives. Serve immediately.

NUTRITION: Calories 100 Fat 2g Protein 5g Carbs 19g

DINNER

Buttered Scallops

Basic Recipe

Preparation Time: 10 minutes **Cooking Time:**
5 minutes **Servings:** 8 **INGREDIENTS:**

- 4 tablespoons butter, melted
- 3-pounds Sea scallops
- 2 tablespoons fresh thyme, minced
- Salt and freshly ground black pepper, to taste

DIRECTIONS:

1. Add butter, sea scallops, thyme, salt and pepper in a bowl. Toss to coat well.
2. Preheat the air fryer to 385 degrees F and grease the air fryer basket.
3. Place scallops in the basket and cook for 5 minutes
4. Take out and serve hot.
5. Tip: Pour melted butter on the scallops to enhance their taste.

NUTRITION: Calories 203 Fat 7.1g Carbs 4.5g Protein 28.7g

Ham Wrapped Prawns

Basic Recipe

Preparation Time: 15 minutes **Cooking Time:**
15 minutes **Servings:** 4 **INGREDIENTS:**

- 2 garlic cloves, minced
- 1 tablespoon paprika
- 8 king prawns, peeled, deveined and chopped
- 4 ham slices, halved
- 2 tablespoons olive oil
- Salt and freshly ground black pepper, to taste

DIRECTIONS:

6. Preheat the air fryer to 430 degrees F and wrap each prawn with a ham slice.
7. Arrange in the air fryer basket and cook for about 4 minutes
8. Dish out and meanwhile place bell pepper in the air fryer basket.
9. Cook for about 10 minutes and transfer in a bowl.
10. Cover the bowl with a foil and set aside for 15 minutes
11. Now, place bell pepper, garlic, paprika and oil in a blender.
12. Blend till a puree is formed and serve with ham wrapped prawns.

NUTRITION: Calories 553 Fat 33.6g Carbs 2.6g Protein 5g

Nacho Chips Crusted Prawns

Basic Recipe

Preparation Time: 10 minutes **Cooking Time:**
10 minutes **Servings:** 8 **INGREDIENTS:**

- 2 large eggs
- 36 prawns, peeled and deveined
- 1½-pounds Nacho flavored chips, crushed finely

DIRECTIONS:

1. Add nacho chips in a bowl and crush well.
2. Add eggs in another bowl and beat well.
3. Preheat the air fryer to 350 degrees F.
4. Dip each prawn in the egg mixture and then in the crushed nachos.
5. Place them in the air fryer and cook for about 8 minutes
6. Take out and serve hot.
7. Tip: More crushed nachos will make prawns crispier.

NUTRITION: Calories 1090 Fat 55.2g Carbs 101.9g Protein 49.2g

Spicy Shrimp

Basic Recipe

Preparation Time: 5 minutes **Cooking Time:** 5 minutes **Servings:** 8 **INGREDIENTS:**

- 2 teaspoons old bay seasoning
- 1 teaspoon cayenne pepper
- 1 teaspoon smoked paprika
- 4 tablespoons olive oil
- 2-pounds tiger shrimp
- Salt, to taste

DIRECTIONS:

1. Add all the ingredients in a large bowl. Mix well. Preheat the air fryer to 390 degrees F and grease the air fryer basket.
2. Place shrimps in the air fryer basket and cook for about 5 minutes. Take out and serve hot.
3. Tip: Top with chili sauce to enhance its taste.

NUTRITION: Calories 174 Fat 8.3g Carbs 0.3g Protein 23.8g

Lemon Tuna

Basic Recipe

Preparation Time: 10 minutes **Cooking Time:** 12 minutes **Servings:** 4 **INGREDIENTS:**

- 1 tablespoon fresh lime juice
- 1 egg
- 3 tablespoons canola oil
- 2 tablespoons hot sauce
- 2 teaspoons Dijon mustard
- 2 tablespoons fresh parsley, chopped
- ½ pound water packed plain tuna
- ½ cup breadcrumbs
- Salt and freshly ground black pepper, to taste

DIRECTIONS:

4. Add tuna fish, parsley, mustard, crumbs, citrus juice and hot sauce in a bowl. Mix well.
5. Now, add oil, salt and eggs in the bowl and make patties from the mixture.
6. Refrigerate and preheat the air fryer to 360 degrees F.
7. Place the patties in the air fryer basket and cook for 12 minutes
8. Take out and serve hot.

NUTRITION: Calories 315 Fat 18.7g Carbs 25g Protein 10.7g

Lemony & Spicy Coconut Crusted Prawns

Basic Recipe

Preparation Time: 20 minutes **Cooking Time:** 7 minutes **Servings:** 4 **INGREDIENTS:**

- ½ cup unsweetened coconut, shredded
- ¼ teaspoon lemon zest
- ¼ teaspoon cayenne pepper
- Vegetable oil, as required
- ¼ teaspoon red pepper flakes, crushed
- ½ cup flour
- ½ cup breadcrumbs
- 1-pound prawns, peeled and de-veined
- 2 egg whites
- Salt and black pepper, to taste

DIRECTIONS:

9. Take a shallow dish and mix salt, flour and pepper in it.
10. Crack eggs in another shallow dish. Beat well.
11. In the third shallow dish, add coconut, breadcrumbs, lime zest, salt and cayenne pepper. Mix well.
12. Now, preheat the air fryer to 395 degrees F.
13. Dip shrimp into flour mixture, then in the egg mixture and roll them evenly into the breadcrumb mixture.
14. Place them in the air fryer basket and Drizzle with vegetable oil over them.
15. Cook for about 7 minutes and take out.
16. Serve and enjoy!

NUTRITION: Calories 773 Fat 60.7g Carbs 25.5g Protein 31.5g

Tuna Stuffed Potatoes

Basic Recipe

Preparation Time: 15 minutes **Cooking Time:** 30 minutes **Servings:** 4 **INGREDIENTS:**

- 1½-pounds tuna, Dry out
- 2 tablespoons plain Greek yogurt
- ½ tablespoon olive oil
- 4 starchy potatoes, soaked for 30 minutes
- 1 tablespoon capers
- 1 teaspoon red chili powder
- 1 scallion, chopped and divided
- Salt and freshly ground black pepper, to taste

DIRECTIONS:

1. Preheat the air fryer to 355 degrees F.
2. Place the potatoes in the air fryer basket and cook for about 30 minutes
3. Take out and place on a flat surface.
4. Meanwhile, add yogurt, tuna, red chili powder, scallion, salt and pepper in a bowl. Mix well.
5. Cut each potato from top side lengthwise and press the open side of potato halves slightly.
6. Stuff potato with tuna mixture and sprinkle with capers.
7. Dish out and serve.

NUTRITION: Calories 1387 Fat 54g Carbs 35.7g Protein 180.7g

Cajun Spiced Salmon

Basic Recipe

Preparation Time: 10 minutes **Cooking Time:** 10 minutes **Servings:** 8 **INGREDIENTS:**

- 4 tablespoons Cajun seasoning
- 4 salmon steaks

DIRECTIONS:

1. Add Cajun seasoning in a bowl and rub salmon evenly with it.
2. Preheat the air fryer to 385 degrees F.
3. Arrange air fryer grill pan and place salmon steaks on it.
4. Cook for about 8 minutes and flip once in the middle way.
5. Take out and serve hot.

NUTRITION: Calories 118 Fat 5.5g Carbs 0g Protein 17.3g

Tangy Salmon

Basic Recipe

Preparation Time: 10 minutes **Cooking Time:**
10 minutes **Servings:** 8 **INGREDIENTS:**

- 4 tablespoons Cajun seasoning
- 8 salmon fillets
- 4 tablespoons fresh lemon juice

DIRECTIONS:

1. Season salmon fillets with Cajun seasoning and set aside for 15 minutes
2. Preheat the air fryer to 360 degrees F and arrange grill pan in it.
3. Place salmon fillets on the grill pan and cook for about 7 minutes
4. Drizzle with lemon juice and serve.

NUTRITION: Calories 237 Fat 11.1g Carbs 21g Protein 34.7g

Sesame Seeds Coated Fish

Basic Recipe

Preparation Time: 20 minutes **Cooking Time:**
20 minutes **Servings:** 28 **INGREDIENTS:**

- ½ cup sesame seeds, toasted
- ½ teaspoon dried rosemary, crushed
- 8 tablespoons olive oil
- 14 frozen fish fillets (white fish of your choice)
- 6 eggs
- ½ cup breadcrumbs
- 8 tablespoons plain flour
- Salt and freshly ground black pepper, to taste

DIRECTIONS:

1. Take three dishes, place flour in one, crack eggs in the other and mix remaining ingredients except fillets in the third one.
2. Now, coat fillets in the flour and dip in the beaten eggs.
3. Then, dredge generously with the sesame seeds mixture.
4. Meanwhile, preheat the air fryer to 390 degrees F and line the air fryer basket with the foil.
5. Arrange fillets in the basket and cook for about 14 minutes, flipping once in the middle way.
6. Take out and serve hot.

NUTRITION: Calories 179 Fat 9.3g Carbs: 15.8g Protein 7.7g

Parsley Catfish

Basic Recipe

Preparation Time: 10 minutes **Cooking Time:**
25 minutes **Servings:** 4 **INGREDIENTS:**

- 4 catfish fillets
- 1/4 cup Louisiana Fish fry
    - 1 tablespoon olive oil
    - 1 tablespoon chopped parsley optional
    - 1 lemon, sliced
    - Fresh herbs, to garnish

DIRECTIONS:

1. Preheat air fryer to 400 degrees F.
2. Rinse the fish fillets and pat them try.
3. Rub the fillets with the seasoning and coat well.
4. Spray oil on top of each fillet.
5. Place the fillets in the air fryer basket.
6. Cover the lid and cook for 10 minutes
7. Flip the fillets and cook more for another 10 minutes
8. Flip the fish and cook for 3 minutes until crispy.
9. Garnish with parsley, fresh herbs, and lemon.
10. Serve warm.

NUTRITION: Calories 248 Fat 15.7 g Carbs 0.4 g Protein
24.9 g

Seasoned Salmon

Basic Recipe

Preparation Time: 5 minutes **Cooking Time:**
10 minutes **Servings:** 4 **INGREDIENTS:**

- 2 wild caught salmon fillets, 1-1/12-inches thick
- 2 teaspoons avocado oil or olive oil
- 2 teaspoons paprika
- Salt and coarse, to taste
- Black pepper, to taste
- Green herbs, to garnish

DIRECTIONS:

1. Clean the salmon and let it rest for 1 hour at room temperature.
2. Season the fish with olive oil, salt, pepper, and paprika.
3. Arrange the fish in the air fryer basket.
4. Cook for 7 minutes at 390 degrees.
5. Once done, remove the fish from the fryer.
6. Garnish with fresh herbs.
7. Serve warm.

NUTRITION: Calories 249 Fat 11.9 g Carbs 1.8 g Protein 35 g

Ranch Fish Fillets

Basic Recipe

Preparation Time: 5 minutes **Cooking Time:**
13 minutes **Servings:** 4 **INGREDIENTS:**

- 3/4 cup breadcrumbs or Panko or crushed cornflakes
- 1 packet dry ranch-style dressing mix
- 2 1/2 tablespoons vegetable oil
- 2 eggs beaten
- 4 tilapia salmon or other fish fillets
- Herbs and chilies to garnish

DIRECTIONS:

1. Preheat the air fryer to 180 degrees F.
2. Mix ranch dressing with panko in a bowl.
3. Whisk eggs in a shallow bowl.
4. Dip each fish fillet in the egg then coat evenly with the panko mixture.
5. Place the fillets in the air fryer.
6. Cook for 13 minutes
7. Serve warm with herbs and chilies.

NUTRITION: Calories 301 Fat 12.2 g Carbs: 15 g Protein
28.8 g

Montreal Fried Shrimp

Basic Recipe

Preparation Time: 5 minutes **Cooking Time:**
10 minutes **Servings:** 6 **INGREDIENTS:**

- 1-pound raw shrimp peeled and deveined
- 1 egg white 3 tablespoon
- 1/2 cup all-purpose flour
- 3/4 cup panko breadcrumbs
- 1 teaspoon paprika
- 1 tablespoon McCormick's Grill Mates Montreal Chicken Seasoning or to taste
- Salt and pepper to taste
- Cooking spray

DIRECTIONS:

1. Preheat the Air Fryer to 400 degrees F.
2. Toss the shrimp with Montreal seasonings.
3. Whisk egg whites in a medium sized bowl.
4. Keep the breadcrumbs and flour in separate bowls.
5. First dredge each shrimp in the flour, then dip into the egg whites, and then coat with the breadcrumbs.
6. Place the coated shrimps in the air dryer and spray the cooking oil over them.
7. Air fry for about 4 minutes then flip the shrimps.
8. Continue cooking for another 4 minutes
9. Serve warm.

NUTRITION: Calories 248 Fat 2.4 g Carbs 12.2 g Protein 44.3 g

Crispy Salt and Pepper Tofu

Basic Recipe

Preparation Time: 5 minutes **Cooking Time:**
20 minutes **Servings:** 4 **INGREDIENTS:**

- ¼ cup chickpea flour
- ¼ cup arrowroot (or cornstarch)
- 1 teaspoon sea salt
- 1 teaspoon granulated garlic
- ½ teaspoon freshly grated black pepper
- 1 (15-ounce) package tofu, firm or extra-firm
- Cooking oil spray (sunflower, safflower, or refined coconut)
- Asian Spicy Sweet Sauce, optional

DIRECTIONS:

1. In a medium bowl, combine the flour, arrowroot, salt, garlic, and pepper. Stir well to combine. Cut the tofu into cubes (no need to press—if it's a bit watery, that's fine!). Place the cubes into the flour mixture. Toss well to coat. Spray the tofu with oil and toss again. (The spray will help the coating better stick to the tofu.)

2. Spray the air fryer basket with the oil. Place the tofu in a single layer in the air fryer basket (you may have to do this in 2 batches, depending on the size of your appliance) and spray the tops with oil. Fry for 8 minutes Remove the air fryer basket and spray again with oil. Toss gently or turn the pieces over. Spray with oil again and fry for another 7 minutes, or until golden-browned and very crisp. Serve immediately, either plain or with the Asian Spicy Sweet Sauce.

NUTRITION: Calories 148 Fat 5g Carbs 14g Protein 11g

Crispy Indian Wrap

Basic Recipe

Preparation Time: 20 minutes **Cooking Time:** 8
minutes **Servings:** 4 **INGREDIENTS:**

- Cilantro Chutney
- 2¾ cups diced potato, cooked until tender
- 2 teaspoons oil (coconut, sunflower, or safflower)
- 3 large garlic cloves, minced or pressed
- 1½ tablespoons fresh lime juice
- 1½ teaspoons cumin powder
- 1 teaspoon onion granules
- 1 teaspoon coriander powder
- ½ teaspoon sea salt
- ½ teaspoon turmeric
- ¼ teaspoon cayenne powder
- 4 large flour tortillas, preferably whole grain or sprouted
- 1 cup cooked garbanzo beans (canned are fine), rinsed and Dry out
- ½ cup finely chopped cabbage
- ¼ cup minced red onion or scallion
- Cooking oil spray (sunflower, safflower, or refined coconut)

DIRECTIONS:

1. Make the Cilantro Chutney and set aside.
2. In a large bowl, mash the potatoes well, using a potato masher or large fork. Add the oil, garlic, lime, cumin, onion, coriander, salt, turmeric, and cayenne. Stir very well, until thoroughly combined. Set aside.
3. Lay the tortillas out flat on the counter. In the middle of each, evenly distribute the potato filling. Add some of the garbanzo beans, cabbage, and red onion to each, on top of the potatoes.
4. Spray the air fryer basket with oil and set aside. Enclose the Indian wraps by folding the bottom of the tortillas up and over the filling, then folding the

   sides in—and finally rolling the bottom up to form, essentially, an enclosed burrito.
5. Place the wraps in the air fryer basket, seam side down. They can touch each other a little bit, but if they're too crowded, you'll need to cook them in batches. Fry for 5 minutes Spray with oil again, flip over, and

cook an additional 2 or 3 minutes, until nicely browned and crisp. Serve topped with the Cilantro Chutney.

NUTRITION: Calories 288 Fat 7g Carbs 50g Protein 9g

Easy Peasy Pizza

Basic Recipe

Preparation Time: 5 minutes **Cooking Time:**
10 minutes **Servings:** 4 **INGREDIENTS:**

- Cooking oil spray (coconut, sunflower, or safflower)
- 1 flour tortilla, preferably sprouted or whole grain
- ¼ cup vegan pizza or marinara sauce
- ⅓Cup grated vegan mozzarella cheese or Cheesy Sauce
- Toppings of your choice

DIRECTIONS:

1. Spray the air fryer basket with oil. Place the tortilla in the air fryer basket. If the tortilla is a little bigger than the base, no problem! Simply fold the edges up a bit to form a semblance of a —crust.|
2. Pour the sauce in the center, and evenly distribute it around the tortilla —crust| (I like to use the back of a spoon for this purpose).
3. Sprinkle evenly with vegan cheese, and add your toppings. Bake it for 9 minutes, or until nicely browned. Remove carefully, cut into four pieces, and enjoy.

NUTRITION: Calories 210 Fat 6g Carbs 33g Protein 5g

Eggplant Parmigiana

Basic Recipe

Preparation Time: 15 minutes **Cooking Time:**
40 minutes **Servings:** 4 **INGREDIENTS:**

- 1 medium eggplant (about 1 pound), sliced into ½- inch-thick rounds
- 2 tablespoons tamari or shoyu
- 3 tablespoons nondairy milk, plain and unsweetened
- 1 cup chickpea flour (see Substitution Tip)
- 1 tablespoon dried basil
- 1 tablespoon dried oregano
- 2 teaspoons garlic granules
- 2 teaspoons onion granules
- ½ teaspoon sea salt
- ½ teaspoons freshly ground black pepper
- Cooking oil spray (sunflower, safflower, or refined coconut)
- Vegan marinara sauce (your choice)
  - Shredded vegan cheese (preferably mozzarella; see Ingredient Tip)

DIRECTIONS:

1. Place the eggplant slices in a large bowl, and pour the tamari and milk over the top. Turn the pieces over to coat them as evenly as possible with the liquids. Set aside.
2. Make the coating: In a medium bowl, combine the flour, basil, oregano, garlic, onion, salt, and pepper and stir well. Set aside.
3. Spray the air fryer basket with oil and set aside.
4. Stir the eggplant slices again and transfer them to a plate (stacking is fine). Do not discard the liquid in the bowl.
5. Bread the eggplant by tossing an eggplant round in the flour mixture. Then, dip in the liquid again. Double up on the coating by placing the eggplant again in the flour mixture, making sure that all sides are nicely breaded. Place in the air fryer basket.
6. Repeat with enough eggplant rounds to make a (mostly) single layer in the air fryer basket. (You'll need to cook it in batches, so that you don't have too much overlap and it cooks perfectly.)
7. Spray the tops of the eggplant with enough oil so that you no longer see dry patches in the coating. Fry for 8 minutes. Remove the air fryer basket

and spray the tops again. Turn each piece over, again taking care not to overlap the rounds too much. Spray the tops with oil, again making sure that no dry patches remain. Fry for another 8 minutes, or until nicely browned and crisp.

8. Repeat steps 5 to 7 one more time, or until all of the eggplant is crisp and browned.

9. Finally, place half of the eggplant in a 6-inch round, 2-inch deep baking pan and top with marinara sauce and a sprinkle of vegan cheese. Fry for 3 minutes, or until the sauce is hot and cheese is melted (be careful not to overcook, or the eggplant edges will burn). Serve immediately, plain or over pasta. Otherwise, you can store the eggplant in the fridge for several days and then make a fresh batch whenever the mood strikes by repeating this step!

NUTRITION: Calories 217 Fat 9g Carbs 38g Protein 9g

Luscious Lazy Lasagna

Basic Recipe

Preparation Time: 15 minutes **Cooking Time:**
15 minutes **Servings:** 4 **INGREDIENTS:**

- 8 ounces lasagna noodles, preferably bean-based, but any kind will do
- 1 tablespoon extra-virgin olive oil
- 2 cups crumbled extra-firm tofu, Dry out and water squeezed out
- 2 cups loosely packed fresh spinach
- 2 tablespoons nutritional yeast
- 2 tablespoons fresh lemon juice
- 1 teaspoon onion granules
- 1 teaspoon sea salt
- ⅛ Teaspoon freshly ground black pepper
- 4 large garlic cloves, minced or pressed
- 2 cups vegan pasta sauce, your choice
- ½ cup shredded vegan cheese (preferably mozzarella)

DIRECTIONS:

1. Cook the noodles until a little firmer than al dente (they'll get a little softer after you air-fry them in the lasagna). Dry out and set aside.
2. While the noodles are cooking, make the filling. In a large pan over medium-high heat, add the olive oil, tofu, and spinach. Stir-fry for a minute, then add the nutritional yeast, lemon juice, onion, salt, pepper, and garlic. Stir well and cook just until the spinach is nicely wilted. Remove from heat.
3. To make half a batch (one 6-inch round, 2-inch deep baking pan) of lasagna: Spread a thin layer of pasta sauce in the baking pan. Layer 2 or 3 lasagna noodles on top of the sauce. Top with a little more sauce and some of the tofu mixture. Place another 2 or 3 noodles on top, and add another layer of sauce and then another layer of tofu. Finish with a layer of noodles, and then a final layer of sauce. Sprinkle about half of the vegan cheese on top (omit if you prefer; see the Ingredient Tip from the Eggplant Parmigiana). Place the pan in the air fryer and Bake it for 15 minutes, or until the noodles are browning around the edges and the cheese is melted. Cut and serve.

NUTRITION: Calories 317 Fat 8g Carbs 46g Protein 20g

Pasta with Creamy Cauliflower Sauce

Basic Recipe

Preparation Time: 10 minutes **Cooking Time:** 20 minutes **Servings:** 4 **INGREDIENTS:**

- 4 cups cauliflower florets
- Cooking oil spray (sunflower,
- Safflower, or refined coconut)
- 1 medium onion, chopped
- 8 ounces pasta, your choice (about 4 cups cooked; use gluten-free pasta if desired)
- Fresh chives or scallion tops, for garnish
- ½ cup raw cashew pieces (see Ingredient Tip)
- 1½ cups water
- 1 tablespoon nutritional yeast
- 2 large garlic cloves, peeled
- 2 tablespoons fresh lemon juice
- 1½ teaspoons sea salt
- ¼ teaspoons freshly ground black pepper

DIRECTIONS:

1. Place the cauliflower in the air fryer basket, sprits the tops with oil spray, and roast for 8 minutes Remove the air fryer basket, stir, and add the onion. Sprits with oil again and roast for another 10 minutes, or until the cauliflower is browned and the onions are tender.
2. While the vegetables are roasting in the air fryer, cook the pasta according to the package directions and mince the chives or scallions. Set aside.
3. In a blender jar, place the roasted cauliflower and onions along with the cashews, water, nutritional yeast, garlic, lemon, salt, and pepper. Blend well, until very smooth and creamy. Serve a generous portion of the sauce on top of the warm pasta, and top with the minced chives or scallions. The sauce will store, refrigerated in an airtight container, for about a week.

NUTRITION: Calories 341 Fat 9g Carbs 51g Protein 14g

Lemony Lentils with "Fried" Onions

Basic Recipe

Preparation Time: 10 minutes **Cooking Time:** 30 minutes **Servings:** 4 **INGREDIENTS:**

- 1 cup red lentils
- 4 cups water
- Cooking oil spray (coconut, sunflower, or safflower)
- 1 medium-size onion, peeled and cut into ¼-inch- thick rings
- Sea salt
- ½ cup kale, stems removed, thinly sliced
- 3 large garlic cloves, pressed or minced
- 2 tablespoons fresh lemon juice
- 2 teaspoons nutritional yeast
- 1 teaspoon sea salt
- 1 teaspoon lemon zest (see Ingredient Tip)
- ¾ teaspoons freshly ground black pepper

DIRECTIONS:

1. In a medium-large pot, bring the lentils and water to a boil over medium-high heat.
2. Reduce the heat to low and simmer, uncovered, for about 30 minutes (or until the lentils have dissolved completely), making sure to stir every 5 minutes or so as they cook (so that the lentils don't stick to the bottom of the pot).
3. While the lentils are cooking, get the rest of your dish together.
4. Spray the air fryer basket with oil and place the onion rings inside, separating them as much as possible. Spray them with the oil and sprinkle with a little salt. Fry for 5 minutes.
5. Remove the air fryer basket, shake or stir, spray again with oil, and fry for another 5 minutes.
6. (Note: You're aiming for all of the onion slices to be crisp and well browned, so if some of the pieces begin to do that, transfer them from the air fryer basket to a plate.)
7. Remove the air fryer basket, spray the onions again with oil, and fry for a final 5 minutes or until all the pieces are crisp and browned.
8. To finish the lentils: Add the kale to the hot lentils, and stir very well, as the heat from the lentils will steam the thinly sliced greens.
9. Stir in the garlic, lemon juice, nutritional yeast, salt, zest, and pepper.

112

10. Stir very well and then distribute evenly in bowls. Top with the crisp onion rings and serve.

NUTRITION: Calories 220 Fat 1g Carbs 39g Protein 15g

Our Daily Bean

Basic Recipe

Preparation Time: 5 minutes **Cooking Time:**
10 minutes **Servings:** 4 **INGREDIENTS:**

- 1 (15-ounce) can pinto beans, Dry out
- ¼ cup tomato sauce
- 2 tablespoons nutritional yeast
- 2 large garlic cloves, pressed or minced
- ½ teaspoon dried oregano
- ½ teaspoon cumin
- ¼ teaspoon sea salt
- ⅛ Teaspoon freshly ground black pepper
- Cooking oil spray (sunflower, safflower, or refined coconut)

DIRECTIONS:

1. In a medium bowl, stir together the beans, tomato sauce, nutritional yeast, garlic, oregano, cumin, salt, and pepper until well combined.
2. Spray the 6-inch round, 2-inch deep baking pan with oil and pour the bean mixture into it. Bake it for 4 minutes Remove, stir well, and Bake it for another 4 minutes, or until the mixture has thickened and is heated through. It will most likely form a little crust on top and be lightly browned in spots. Serve hot. This will keep, refrigerated in an airtight container, for up to a week.

NUTRITION: Calories 284 Fat 4g Carbs 47g Protein 20g

Taco Salad with Creamy Lime Sauce

Basic Recipe

Preparation Time: 10 minutes **Cooking Time:**
10 minutes **Servings:** 4 **INGREDIENTS:**
For The Sauce

- 1 (12.3-ounce) package of silken-firm tofu
- ¼ cup plus 1 tablespoon fresh lime juice
- Zest of 1 large lime (1 teaspoon)
- 1½ tablespoons coconut sugar
- 3 large garlic cloves, peeled
- 1 teaspoon sea salt
- ½ teaspoon ground chipotle powder For The Salad
- 6 cups romaine lettuce, chopped (1 large head)

  - 1 (15-ounce) can vegan refried beans (or whole pinto or black beans if you prefer)
  - 1 cup chopped red cabbage
  - 2 medium tomatoes, chopped
  - ½ cup chopped cilantro
  - ¼ cup minced scallions
  - Double batch of garlic lime tortilla chips

DIRECTIONS:

1. To Make the Sauce
2. Dry out the tofu (pour off any liquid) and place in a blender.
3. Add the lime juice and zest, coconut sugar, garlic, salt, and chipotle powder. Blend until very smooth. Set aside.
4. To Make the Salad
5. Distribute the lettuce equally into three big bowls.
6. In a small pan over medium heat, warm the beans, stirring often, until hot (this should take less than a minute). Place on top of the lettuce.
7. Top the beans with the cabbage, tomatoes, cilantro, and scallions.
8. Drizzle with generously with the Creamy Lime Sauce and serve with the double batch of air-fried chips. Enjoy immediately.

NUTRITION: Calories 422 Fat 7g Carbs 71g Protein 22g

BBQ Jackfruit Nachos

Basic Recipe

Preparation Time: 30 minutes **Cooking Time:** 20 minutes **Servings:** 4 **INGREDIENTS:**

- 1 (20-ounce) can jackfruit, dry out
- ⅓ cup prepared vegan bbq sauce
- ¼ cup water
- 2 tablespoons tamari or shoyu
- 1 tablespoon fresh lemon juice
- 4 large garlic cloves, pressed or minced
- 1 teaspoon onion granules
- ⅛ Teaspoon cayenne powder
- ⅛ Teaspoon liquid smoke
- Double batch garlic lime tortilla chips
- 2½ cups prepared cheesy sauce
- 3 medium-size tomatoes, chopped
- ¾ cup guacamole of your choice
- ¾ cup chopped cilantro
- ½ cup minced red onion
- 1 jalapeño, seeds removed and thinly sliced (optional)

DIRECTIONS:

1. In a large skillet over high heat, place the jackfruit, BBQ sauce, water, tamari, lemon juice, garlic, onion granules, cayenne, and liquid smoke. Stir well and break up the jackfruit a bit with a spatula.
2. Once the mixture boils, reduce the heat to low. Continue to cook, stirring often (and breaking up the jackfruit as you stir), for about 20 minutes, or

    until all of the liquid has been absorbed. Remove from the heat and set aside.
3. Assemble the nachos: Distribute the chips onto three plates, and then top evenly with the jackfruit mixture, warmed Cheesy Sauce, tomatoes, guacamole, cilantro, onion, and jalapeño (if using). Enjoy immediately, because soggy chips are tragic.

NUTRITION: Calories 661 Fat 15g Carbs 124g Protein 22g

10-Minute Chimichanga

Basic Recipe

Preparation Time: 5 minutes **Cooking Time:** 10 minutes **Servings:** 4 **INGREDIENTS:**

- 1 whole-grain tortilla
- ½ cup vegan refried beans
- ¼ cup grated vegan cheese (optional)
- Cooking oil spray (sunflower, safflower, or refined coconut)
- ½ cup fresh salsa (or Green Chili Sauce)
- 2 cups chopped romaine lettuce (about ½ head)
- Guacamole (optional)
- Chopped cilantro (optional)
- Cheesy Sauce (optional)

DIRECTIONS:

4. Lay the tortilla on a flat surface and place the beans in the center. Top with the cheese, if using. Wrap the bottom up over the filling, and then fold in the sides. Then roll it all up so as to enclose the beans inside the tortilla (you're making an enclosed burrito here).
5. Spray the air fryer basket with oil, place the tortilla wrap inside the basket, seam-side down, and spray the top of the chimichanga with oil. Fry for 5 minutes Spray the top (and sides) again with oil, flip over, and spray the other side with oil. Fry for an additional 2 or 3 minutes, until nicely browned and crisp.
6. Transfer to a plate. Top with the salsa, lettuce, guacamole, cilantro, and/or Cheesy Sauce, if using. Serve immediately.

NUTRITION: Calories 317 Fat 6g Carbs 55g Protein 13g

Mexican Stuffed Potatoes

Intermediate Recipe Preparation Time: 15 minutes **Cooking Time:** 40 minutes **Servings:** 4

INGREDIENTS:

- 4 large potatoes, any variety (I like Yukon Gold or russets for this dish; see Cooking Tip)
- Cooking oil spray (sunflower, safflower, or refined coconut)
- 1½ cups Cheesy Sauce
- 1 cup black or pinto beans (canned beans are fine; be sure to Dry out and rinse)
- 2 medium tomatoes, chopped
- 1 scallion, finely chopped
- ⅓Cup finely chopped cilantro
- 1 jalapeño, finely sliced or minced (optional)
- 1 avocado, diced (optional)

DIRECTIONS:

1. Scrub the potatoes, prick with a fork, and spray the outsides with oil. Place in the air fryer (leaving room in between so the air can circulate) and Bake it for 30 minutes
2. While the potatoes are cooking, prepare the Cheesy Sauce and additional items. Set aside.
3. Check the potatoes at the 30-minute mark by poking a fork into them. If they're very tender, they're done. If not, continue to cook until a fork inserted proves them to be well-done. (As potato sizes vary, so will your cook time—the average cook time is usually about 40 minutes)
4. When the potatoes are getting very close to being tender, warm the Cheesy Sauce and the beans in separate pans.
5. To assemble: Plate the potatoes and cut them across the top. Then, pry them open with a fork— just enough to get all the goodies in there. Top each potato with the Cheesy Sauce, beans, tomatoes, scallions, cilantro, and jalapeño and avocado, if using. Enjoy immediately.

NUTRITION: Calories 420 Fat 5g Carbs 80g Fiber 17g Protein 15g

Kids" Taquitos

Basic Recipe

Preparation Time: 5 minutes **Cooking Time:** 10
minutes **Servings:** 4 **INGREDIENTS:**

- 8 corn tortillas
- Cooking oil spray (coconut, sunflower, or safflower)
- 1 (15-ounce) can vegan refried beans
- 1 cup shredded vegan cheese
- Guacamole (optional)
- Cheesy Sauce (optional)
- Vegan sour cream (optional)
- Fresh salsa (optional)

DIRECTIONS:

7. Warm the tortillas (so they don't break): Run them under water for a second, and then place in an oil- sprayed air fryer basket (stacking them is fine). Fry for 1 minute.

8. Remove to a flat surface, laying them out individually. Place an equal amount of the beans in a line down the center of each tortilla. Top with the vegan cheese.

9. Roll the tortilla sides up over the filling and place seam-side down in the air fryer basket (this will help them seal so the tortillas don't fly open). Add just enough to fill the basket without them touching too

   much (you may need to do another batch, depending on the size of your air fryer basket).

10. Spray the tops with oil. Fry for 7 minutes, or until the tortillas are golden-brown and lightly crisp. Serve immediately with your preferred toppings.

NUTRITION: Calories 286 Fat 9g Carbs 44g Protein 9g

Immune-Boosting Grilled Cheese Sandwich

Basic Recipe

Preparation Time: 5 minutes **Cooking Time:**
15 minutes **Servings:** 4 **INGREDIENTS:**

- 2 slices sprouted whole-grain bread (or substitute a gluten-free bread)
- 1 teaspoon vegan margarine or neutral-flavored oil (sunflower, safflower, or refined coconut)
- 2 slices vegan cheese (Violife cheddar or Chao creamy original) or Cheesy Sauce
- 1 teaspoon mellow white miso
- 1 medium-large garlic clove, pressed or finely minced
- 2 tablespoons fermented vegetables, kimchi, or sauerkraut
- Romaine or green leaf lettuce

DIRECTIONS:

11. Spread the outsides of the bread with the vegan margarine. Place the sliced cheese inside and close the sandwich back up again (buttered sides facing out). Place the sandwich in the air fryer basket and fry for 6 minutes Flip over and fry for another 6 minutes, or until nicely browned and crisp on the outside.

12. Transfer to a plate. Open the sandwich and evenly spread the miso and garlic clove over the inside of one of the bread slices. Top with the fermented vegetables and lettuce, close the sandwich back up, cut in half, and serve immediately.

NUTRITION: Calories 288 Fat 13g Carbs 34g Protein 8g

Tamale Pie with Cilantro Lime Cornmeal Crust

Basic Recipe

Preparation Time: 25 minutes **Cooking Time:**
20 minutes **Servings:** 4 **INGREDIENTS:**
For the filling

- 1 medium zucchini, diced (1¼ cups)
- 2 teaspoons   neutral-flavored oil   (sunflower, safflower, or refined coconut)
- 1 cup cooked pinto beans, Dry out
- 1 cup canned diced tomatoes (unsalted) with juice
- 3 large garlic cloves, minced or pressed
- 1 tablespoon chickpea flour
- 1 teaspoon dried oregano
- 1 teaspoon onion granules

    - ½ teaspoon salt
    - ½ teaspoon crushed red chili flakes
    - Cooking oil spray (sunflower, safflower, or refined coconut)

For the crust

    - ½ cup yellow cornmeal, finely ground
    - 1½ cups water
    - ½ teaspoon salt
    - 1 teaspoon nutritional yeast
    - 1 teaspoon   neutral-flavored oil   (sunflower, safflower, or refined coconut)
    - 2 tablespoons finely chopped cilantro
    - ½ teaspoon lime zest

DIRECTIONS:

13. To make the filling
14. In a large skillet set to medium-high heat, sauté the zucchini and oil for 3 minutes or until the zucchini begins to brown.
15. Add the beans, tomatoes, garlic, flour, oregano, onion, salt, and chili flakes to the mixture. Cook it over medium heat, stirring often, for 5 minutes, or until the mixture is thickened and no liquid remains. Remove

121

from the heat.

16. Spray a 6-inch round, 2-inch deep baking pan with oil and place the mixture in the bottom. Smooth out the top and set aside.

17. To make the crust

18. In a medium pot over high heat, place the cornmeal, water, and salt. Whisk constantly as you bring the mixture to a boil. Once it boils, reduce the heat to very low. Add the nutritional yeast and oil and continue to cook, stirring very often, for 10 minutes or until the mixture is very thick and hard to whisk. Remove from the heat.

19. Stir the cilantro and lime zest into the cornmeal mixture until thoroughly combined. Using a rubber spatula, gently spread it evenly onto the filling in the baking pan to form a smooth crust topping. Place in the air fryer basket and Bake it for 20 minutes, or until the top is golden-brown. Let it cool for 5 to 10 minutes, then cut and serve.

NUTRITION: Calories 165 Fat 5g Carbs 26g Protein 6g

CPSIA information can be obtained
at www.ICGtesting.com
Printed in the USA
BVHW071926130421
604819BV00008BA/814